Praise for *At Larg*

"Sparkling . . . These essays . . . [?] man's intellect and curiosity . . [?] handshakes, but they quickly distill into murmurs floating across the table during a long afternoon squandered over Earl Grey and blueberry scones with a sympathetic, playfully erudite and hilariously self-deprecating friend."
—Margaria Fichtner, *The Miami Herald*

"As it would be impractical for Fadiman to invite all her admiring readers over for dinner and lively conversation, her book will have to satisfy us. And it does."
—Brigitte Frase, *Star Tribune* (Minneapolis)

"Across the Atlantic, the endurance of a literary magazine culture ensures the survival of the [essay] genre, with Anne Fadiman as one of its most distinguished practitioners."
—Jonathan Keates, *The Times Literary Supplement*

"Pleasures both sensuous and brainy inspire Anne Fadiman's playful and erudite essays. Her delight in language is evident in each avidly crafted sentence . . . She creates a refuge far from the madding crowd, where the past remains vital, where brilliantly hued words pulse as breathtakingly as butterflies, where agility of thought, impeccable syntax, mischievous wit and rarefied knowledge are valued."
—Donna Seaman, *Los Angeles Times Book Review*

"A master of the tangential, a close observer, and a lover of language, Fadiman is blithely brilliant in her pursuit of beauty and meaning as she wrestles with questions of life, death, and rebirth."   —*Booklist*

"Fadiman, owing largely to a colloquial and easy style, transforms the reader into something like a soul mate . . . Fadiman's seemingly effortless prose, a fluent mix of the profound and the buoyant, is captivating, elegant and thought-provoking . . . It's great fun to be in her company."
—Ann Begley, *America*

"A modern spin on the familiar essay gives *At Large* its engaging mixture of intellectual exploration, textured storytelling and accessible prose . . . [Fadiman's] writing maintains a consistent and inviting lucidity. Like writers such as John McPhee or E. B. White, Fadiman has mastered the art of the amble. Her language unfolds with the ebb and flow of conversation, one you can't help but get swept up in."
—Kelly McMasters, *Time Out New York*

" 'Delightful' and 'erudite' aren't words that often go together. But . . . Fadiman finds a way to be both in her enchanting new volume of essays."
—Jane Black, *Boston Magazine*

"Fadiman is utterly delightful, witty and curious, and she's such a stellar writer that if she wrote about pencil shavings, you'd read it aloud to all your friends."
—Lucia Silva, *NPR*'s "Booksellers' Picks for the Beach—or the Backyard"

"To those who have read her work, Anne Fadiman is the object of cultish devotion."

—Robert McCrum, *The Observer* (London)

"Like her hero, Charles Lamb, Fadiman is the very best kind of conversationalist: graceful, perpetually attentive, digressive, precise and, frequently, amused."

—Susannah Herbert, *The Sunday Times* (London)

" 'I believe the survival of the familiar essay is worth fighting for,' [Fadiman] proclaims, and then she writes her heart out to ensure it will endure."

—Richard Grayson, *The Quarterly Conversation*

"These are wonderful essays. The writing is effortless, elegant, and clear, the subjects delightful or weighty or both. Anne Fadiman had me completely charmed by page four."   —Ian Frazier

"Anne Fadiman wins our attention by directing hers with unwavering focus at the world around her. Her perceptions are astute, and her sensibility is so rich and sane, no calculation could violate it. The personal essay was invented so that writers like Fadiman could practice it."

—Sven Birkerts

"Limpid, learned, perspicacious—and relentless. Whatever the subject, Anne Fadiman overlooks nothing, imparts everything, and leaves you wanting more."

—Thomas Mallon

Connie Miller

ANNE FADIMAN

At Large and At Small

Anne Fadiman was born in New York City and was raised in Connecticut and Los Angeles. After graduating from Harvard, she worked as a wilderness instructor in Wyoming before returning to New York to write. She has been a staff writer at *Life*, editor-at-large of *Civilization*, and editor of *The American Scholar*. Her first book, *The Spirit Catches You and You Fall Down* (FSG, 1997), won the National Book Critics Circle Award for general nonfiction. Fadiman is also the author of *Ex Libris* (FSG, 1998) and the editor of *Rereadings* (FSG, 2005). She now lives with her family in western Massachusetts and serves as the Francis Writer-in-Residence at Yale.

ALSO BY ANNE FADIMAN

The Spirit Catches You and You Fall Down

Ex Libris

EDITED BY ANNE FADIMAN

The Best American Essays 2003

Rereadings

AT LARGE

AND AT SMALL

AT LARGE

AND AT SMALL

FAMILIAR ESSAYS BY

ANNE FADIMAN

FARRAR, STRAUS AND GIROUX   NEW YORK

Farrar, Straus and Giroux
18 West 18th Street, New York 10011

Distributed in Canada by Douglas & McIntyre Ltd.
Printed in the United States of America
Published in 2007 by Farrar, Straus and Giroux
First paperback edition, 2008

With the exception of "Under Water," an earlier version of which appeared in *The New Yorker*, the essays in this book appeared, in somewhat different form, in *The American Scholar*.

The Library of Congress has cataloged the hardcover edition as follows:
Fadiman, Anne, 1953–
    At large and at small : familiar essays / by Anne Fadiman.
    p.   cm.
    ISBN-13: 978-0-374-10662-1 (alk. paper)
    ISBN-10: 0-374-10662-2 (alk. paper)
    I. Title.

PS3556.A314Z46 2007
814'.54—dc22

                                                    2006038262

        Paperback ISBN-13: 978-0-374-53131-7
        Paperback ISBN-10: 0-374-53131-5

Designed by Jonathan D. Lippincott

www.fsgbooks.com

7   9   10   8

FOR KIM

Collector of Tiger Swallowtails,

Emperor of Ice Cream

Contents

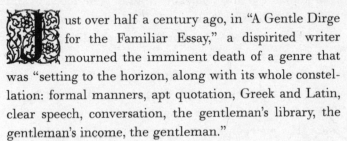ust over half a century ago, in "A Gentle Dirge for the Familiar Essay," a dispirited writer mourned the imminent death of a genre that was "setting to the horizon, along with its whole constellation: formal manners, apt quotation, Greek and Latin, clear speech, conversation, the gentleman's library, the gentleman's income, the gentleman."

The writer was my father, Clifton Fadiman, who—accompanied by his mailbox, his wastebasket, and his insomnia—makes cameo appearances in several of the essays in this book. "A Gentle Dirge for the Familiar Essay" *is* a familiar essay, and it therefore vibrates with a Chinese-box-like meta-ness. Its own excellence fights against its message.

The essay portending the end of the essay has become a genre in itself, one whose persistence suggests that the previous soothsayers may have been wrong and the current ones may therefore be wrong as well. Although most of the items on my father's valedictory list have crept even farther toward the horizon, the most important among them is still in full view. I refer, of course, to conversation, a taste I acquired, along with a fondness for pungent curries and moldering Stilton, at the Fadiman dinner table. Conversation was at the center of my father's life, it's at the center of mine, and it's at the center of the familiar essay.

"Familiar essay" isn't a term one hears often these days. The genre's heyday was the early nineteenth century, when Charles Lamb was dreaming up *The Essays of Elia* under the influence of brandy and tobacco and William Hazlitt was dashing off *Table-Talk* under the influence of strong tea. The familiar essayist didn't speak to the millions; he spoke to *one* reader, as if the two of them were sitting side by side in front of a crackling fire with their cravats loosened, their favorite stimulants at hand, and a long evening of conversation stretching before them. His viewpoint was subjective, his frame of reference concrete, his style digressive, his eccentricities conspicuous, and his laughter usually at his own expense. And though he wrote about himself, he also wrote about a *subject*, something with which he was so familiar, and about which he was often so enthusiastic, that his words were suffused with a lover's intimacy. Hence the profusion of titles beginning with the word "On": "On the Melancholy of Tailors," "On the Feeling of Immortality in Youth," "On the Danger of Confounding Moral with Personal Deformity," "On the Conversation of Authors," "On the Genius and Character of Hogarth," "On the Inconveniences Resulting from Being Hanged," "On the

Custom of Hissing at the Theatres," "On the Love of Life," "On Gusto." On gusto! The familiar essay in a nutshell!

Today's readers encounter plenty of critical essays (more brain than heart) and plenty of personal—very personal—essays (more heart than brain), but not many familiar essays (equal measures of both). If I were to turn Lamb's 1821 "Chapter on Ears" into a twenty-first-century critical essay, I might write about postmodern audiological imagery in the early works of Barbara Cartland. If I were to write a twenty-first-century personal essay, I might tell you about the pimple on my left earlobe that I failed to cover with makeup at my senior prom, about that ear thing my college boyfriend did with his tongue (how did he get it so *pointy?*), and about the countless times I courted deafness by turning up "Jumpin' Jack Flash" to max volume. But I don't want to write—or read—either of those essays. I prefer Lamb's original, which is mostly about his musical ineptitude but also about the sounds of harpsichords, pianos, operatic voices, crowded streets, and carpenter's hammers: in other words, about the author but also about the world.

I believe the survival of the familiar essay is worth fighting for. This little volume is my contribution to the war effort, both a declaration of my esteem—no, my love—for the genre and an expression of my own character, a blend of narcissism and curiosity that is inconvenient in many contexts but perhaps oddly suited to this one. Its dozen essays took shape over the course of seven years, beginning in 1998, and, aside from the last one, they are presented in the order in which they were written. Some were prompted by events in my life (learning to use e-mail, moving from the city to the country), some by events in the larger world (the Culture Wars, which I wrote about while their casualties were still mounting; America's rediscovery of its flag, which I wrote about three months after 9/11). I've left the time-anchored vantage points unchanged. Several of the essays were written under the influence, though not of brandy, tobacco, or tea. I ingested a shocking amount of Häagen-Dazs while I wrote about ice cream. I sustained a terrific caffeine buzz while I wrote about coffee. I wrote every word of the night-owl essay between midnight and dawn. Three essays were composed under the influence of great men: Vilhjalmur Stefansson, Samuel Taylor Coleridge, and—closest to my heart—Charles Lamb, whose shade watched over me, I liked to think, as I sat at my desk and addressed the kind of reader with whom he used to converse himself.

The title is meant to suggest that my interests are presbyopic ("at large") but my focus is myopic ("at small"). While I was working on this book, I came across "On Great and Little Things," an essay by Hazlitt. "The organs of the mind, like the pupil of the eye, may be contracted or dilated to view a broader or narrower surface," he wrote, "and yet find sufficient variety to occupy its attention in each." I couldn't agree more.

Unlike my father, I do not believe that the ability to write a familiar essay depends on whether one's manners are formal (mine aren't), one knows Greek and Latin

(I've forgotten the little I once knew), or one is a gentle-man (I most assuredly am not). If a psychologist were to analyze my attachment to the genre, he might zero in on another Clifton Fadiman passage, one that observes that few women write familiar essays because "the form does not attract them." Well, it attracts *me*. And I hope that it will continue to attract enough other writers—and read-ers—that no dirge, gentle or otherwise, need ever be sung to lament its passing.

A.F.

AT LARGE

AND AT SMALL

COLLECTING NATURE

The net was green. The handle was wood, and the grip was uncomfortably thick, like that of a tennis racket borrowed from an older player. The mesh bag was long enough that if we caught a tiger swallowtail—or a spicebush swallowtail, or a mourning cloak, or a European cabbage, or a common sulphur, or a red admiral, or a painted lady, or a monarch, or a viceroy—we could, with a twist of the wrist, flip its tapered tip over the wire rim and trap the butterfly inside.

Then, being careful not to scrape off the colored scales, we pinched the wings shut and transferred the butterfly to the killing jar. (Our bible, *A Field Guide to the Butterflies of North America, East of the Great Plains*, by Alexander B. Klots, recommended a more complicated method of transfer that involved holding the handle between one's thighs, grasping the bag just below the butterfly, slipping the jar into the net, and coaxing the butterfly into the jar. But this technique demanded a prodigious level of coordination—on the order, say, of that displayed by the Cat in the Hat when he balanced a goldfish bowl on an umbrella while standing on a rubber ball—and we were never able to master it.) My brother and I had started with a shallow plastic container, like a petri dish, which came in the children's butterfly kit that we had rapidly outgrown, but because the hindwing projections of the swallowtails tended to get crushed against the perimeter, we graduated to a large glass jar from which our mother had scrubbed the last traces of strawberry jam. At the bottom of the killing jar was a piece of cotton saturated with carbon tetrachloride.

"Carbon tet," we called it, not because it was easier to pronounce—we shared a weakness for long words—but because the nickname suggested that we and it were on familiar terms, as was indeed the case. Thirty years later, a friend of mine dabbed some spot remover on a sofa, and I instantly recognized the smell of the killing jar. During the fifties, when my brother and I started chasing butterflies, potassium cyanide was still in use as well, but because it is a deadly poison, Professor Klots recommended liquid carbon tetrachloride, which is "not very poisonous unless inhaled deeply," and which we persuaded our parents was as innocuous as smelling salts. The butterfly would flutter for a few moments, sink to the bottom of the jar, and slowly expire.

The murder was less grisly than it would have been in, say, 1810, when insect collectors stabbed their specimens with pins, asphyxiated them over the flames of sulphur matches, and skewered them with red-hot wires.

Around 1820, the vogue in Europe was the "stifling box," a sealed container submerged in boiling water. The killing jar was introduced in the 1850s, after the royal physician used chloroform to ease the delivery of Queen Victoria's eighth child, and net-wielding country vicars across Great Britain realized they could amass their collections of marbled whites and Camberwell beauties without overt violence. They could simply anesthetize their specimens to death.

The problem with chloroform, as with potassium cyanide and carbon tetrachloride, is that these poisons freeze the butterfly's muscles into an extreme version of rigor mortis, and the wings cannot be spread. My brother and I therefore popped the corpse into a "relaxing jar"— now there's a euphemism right up there with Orwell's Ministry of Peace—that dampened it into pliancy, whereupon it could be pinned to the spreading board, a balsa rectangle with a groove down the center that allowed the wings to be flattened without squashing the thorax and abdomen. Caught, killed, relaxed, and spread, the butterfly was laid to rest in a Riker mount, a shallow glass-topped box filled with absorbent cotton—a sort of mass grave for soldiers who had given their lives on the battlefields of suburban Connecticut.

When did we realize that this was horrible? My brother, Kim, and I had started collecting butterflies when he was eight and I was six. Shame set in about two years later. I remember a period of painful overlap, when the light of decency was dawning but the lure of sin was still irresistible. Like alcohol, nicotine, or heroin, lepi-

doptery is hard to renounce. A tiger swallowtail is an un-
believable thing to find in your backyard: a *big* butterfly,
five inches across, striated with yellow and black, with
blue splotches on the hindwings rendered iridescent by
light-diffracting scales—"like the colors," wrote Professor Klots in a memorably lyrical passage, "produced by a
glass prism, the blue of the sky, the spectrum of the rain-
bow, and an oil film on water." Who would not wish to
take such a creature home? To glimpse something so
gaudily tropical, more like a quetzal than a sparrow, on
your own home ground; to pursue it across the lawn,
down the stone steps, around the two topiary peacocks
that stood guard over the wading pool, and along the
flower border, until it lit on a phlox or a zinnia; to swoop
your net through the air and see something fluttering inside; to snatch that bit of life from the rich chaos of nature into your own comparatively lackluster world, which
it instantly brightened and enlarged; to look it up in
Klots and name it and *know* it—well, after you did that a
few times, it was hard to muster much enthusiasm for
Parcheesi.

"The next two days were so wet and windy that there
was no going out," wrote Alfred Russel Wallace in 1869,
about a collecting trip to the Aru Islands, north of Australia:

> [B]ut on the succeeding one the sun shone brightly, and I
> had the good fortune to capture one of the most magnifi-

cent insects the world contains, the great bird-winged butterfly, Ornithoptera poseidon. I trembled with excitement
as I saw it coming majestically towards me, and could
hardly believe I had really succeeded in my stroke till I had
taken it out of the net and was gazing, lost in admiration, at
the velvet black and brilliant green of its wings, seven
inches across, its golden body, and crimson breast. It is true
I had seen similar insects in cabinets at home, but it is quite
another thing to capture such oneself—to feel it struggling
between one's fingers, and to gaze upon its fresh and living
beauty, a bright gem shining out amid the silent gloom of a
dark and tangled forest. The village of Dobbo held that
evening at least one contented man.

Few people read Wallace anymore, even though he
founded the science of island biogeography and, inde-
pendent of Darwin, evolved a theory of natural selection.
A few years ago, I borrowed a 1902 edition of one of his
books from a large university library and noticed that it
had last been checked out in 1949. But he has long been a
favorite of mine, in part because no one has ever done a
better job of capturing the euphoria of netting a really
beautiful specimen. And unlike the editor of a 1975 book
on butterflies—who, when he quoted this passage, squea-
mishly omitted the phrase "to feel it struggling between
one's fingers"—Wallace made no bones about how crucial the violence was to the thrill.

While Wallace was chasing butterflies in the Malay
Archipelago, thousands of his compatriots were doing
the same thing back home in England. A special butterfly
net was even invented that, when folded, looked exactly
like an umbrella, so that one could take it on a stroll

without attracting undue attention. (As the British historian David Elliston Allen has pointed out, one did look rather a fool if it started to rain and one's umbrella remained obstinately furled.) Sunday afternoons, after church, were a favorite time for entomology, which was considered a high-mindedly Christian pursuit. An 1843 pamphlet titled *Instructions for Collecting, Rearing, and Preserving British & Foreign Insects*—it now reposes in an envelope in the Library of Congress, as fragile as a sheaf of butterfly wings—begins with the following words:

> The contemplation of the works of the CREATOR is the highest delight of the rational mind. In them we read, as in a volume fraught with endless wonders, the unlimited power and goodness of that Being, who, in the formation of Atoms, and of Worlds, has alike displayed unfathomable Wisdom. There are few objects in Nature which raise the mind to a higher degree of admiration, than the Insect creation. Their immense numbers—endless variety of form—astonishing metamorphoses—exceeding beauty—the amazing minuteness of some, and the complex and wonderful organization of others, far exceeding that of the higher animals—all tend to prove an Almighty artificer, and inspire astonishment and awe!

I sympathize with these views. When I was in high school, a churchgoing friend attempted to rouse me from my agnosticism by asking, "Isn't there *anything* that seems so miraculous it simply has to be by design?" I answered, "Butterfly metamorphosis." I knew it could be explained by rational principles, but it still seemed to hold an irreducible spark of divinity. When Brahma watched the caterpillars in his vegetable garden change into pupae, and thence into butterflies, he was filled with the certainty that he, too, would attain perfection in a future incarnation. Brahma, however, was content to observe the works of the Creator, whereas the author of the 1843 pamphlet (using methods he detailed in a thirteen-page chapter called "On killing and preserving Insects in general") believed he could appreciate them most fully only if he did them in.

Any parent of a small child is familiar with the impulse to own that which one admires. It is why my husband and I used to tell our daughter, before she was too old to be so easily duped, that FAO Schwarz was a toy *museum*. When we were very young, my brother and I could not yet divorce our ardor for butterflies from our desire to flatten them in Riker mounts and hang them on the wall. Distinguishing the two required an unchildlike conjunction of self-control and guilt: the sort of moral conversion, for example, that might transform a trophy hunter into a wildlife photographer. We threw away our killing jar not because we wished to stop causing pain—crushing an ant or a cockroach, which presumably had a nervous system similar to that of a tiger swallowtail, stirred few qualms—but because, unlike Alfred Russel Wallace, we grew uneasy with the pleasure it gave us.

During the period of withdrawal, when we still caught butterflies but were ashamed of enjoying it, a luna moth settled on the grille of the air conditioner that was bolted into the window of our father's dressing room, on the second floor of our house. If you have ever seen a luna moth—pale green, hindwings tapering to long slender tails, antennae like golden feathers—you have not forgotten it. It was a hot, humid, firefly-filled summer night, and Kim and I were sitting outside on the front lawn. The light from the house illuminated the moth with a spectral glow. We could not reach it from the ground. We could not open the window from inside. I cannot remember ever desiring anything so much.

Aside from the fact that I did not grow up to be a serial killer, my future character was already present, in chrysalid form, in the six-year-old girl who wielded the green butterfly net. She was shy, cerebral, and fussy, the sort of child better liked by adults than by other children; she was obsessed by nomenclature; she derived a false but pleasant sense of competence from mastering lepidoptery's ancillary gear; her conception of nature was incorrigibly romantic; she was painfully affected by beauty; she was a compulsive arranger; she focused on small details—the precise curve of a mourning cloak's forewing, the exact shade of the red spot on a zebra swallowtail's hindwing—rather than on larger and more important questions of behavior and habitat. Although she now collects books instead of butterflies, I cannot say that the intervening thirty-eight years have changed her much.

All children collect things, of course, but the difference between collecting stamps and collecting butterflies is that you do not have to kill the stamps. Also—and this casts lepidoptery in a slightly more favorable light—the rarity of certain species of insects can be naturally experienced, whereas the rarity of stamps must be looked up in a book. A child knows that a common sulphur is less precious than a luna moth because she has seen thousands of the former and only one of the latter, but how could she guess that an 1856 British one-penny rose is worth a dollar and an 1856 British Guiana one-penny magenta is worth $935,000?

I once read a book on collecting that included photographs of collectors of toilet paper, Weetabix boxes, and airsickness bags. They were all male and all nerdy-looking. My father's first cousin, William James Sidis—a child prodigy who learned Latin and Greek at three, entered Harvard at eleven, and ended up an ill-paid back-office clerk—collected streetcar transfers, of which he eventually accumulated more than two thousand. Billy Sidis was nerdy, too, as well as deeply unhappy. Surely the desire to collect inanimate objects with no intrinsic beauty or meaning, as opposed to paintings or books or antique Chinese snuff bottles, reflects a yawning lack of self-confidence. All collecting is a form of spuriously easy mastery, but it is almost unbearably pathetic that a man of Sidis's ability was so incapable, in either his work or his hobby, of picking something anywhere near his own size.

Collecting insects is less pathetic than collecting streetcar transfers, but most people would consider it more sinister. Is it surprising that the revolutionist Jean-Paul Marat, the author of a 1790 pamphlet advocating that "five or six hundred heads be cut off," was an amateur lepidopterist? Is it entirely a coincidence that Alfred Kinsey, before he collected eighteen thousand sexual histories (along with innumerable nudist magazines, pornographic statues, and pieces of sadomasochistic paraphernalia), collected tens of thousands of gall wasps? Was it not inevitable that John Fowles should have made Frederick Clegg, who collected a beautiful art student and imprisoned her in his cellar, a collector of butterflies as well? I read *The Collector* when I was sixteen, and I got a perverse insider's kick when Frederick drugged Miranda with chloroform and carbon tetrachloride, both of which he had previously used in his killing bottle to drug fritillaries and blues.

But on the other side of the scale—and I believe he carries enough weight to outbalance an entire army of lepidopteran weirdos—there is Vladimir Nabokov. It is my view that if you have never netted a butterfly, you cannot truly understand Nabokov. (This, of course, may be merely a rationalization, the ignoble offspring of my desire to believe that the tiger swallowtails of my misspent youth did not die in vain.) Only Nabokov, eloping at age ten with a nine-year-old girl in Biarritz, would have taken, as the sum total of his luggage, a folding butterfly net in a brown paper bag. Nabokov chased butterflies on two continents for six decades; spent seven years as a research fellow in entomology at Harvard, where, during the course of his taxonomic studies, he permanently damaged his vision by spending long hours looking through a microscope at dissected butterfly genitalia; discovered several new species and subspecies, including *Cyclargus erembis* Nabokov and *Neonympha maniola* Nabokov; and wrote twenty-two articles on lepidoptera, including a 1951 review of my own Alexander B. Klots in *The New York Times Book Review*. He called it "wonderfully stimulating." (He did not mention page 164, where, under the heading "*Genus* Lycæides *Scudder*: The Orange Margined Blues," Klots wrote, "The recent work of Nabokov has entirely rearranged the classification of this genus." Years after the publication of *Lolita, Pnin,* and *Pale Fire,* Nabokov took a copy of Klots from his shelf, showed a visitor that sentence, and said, "That's real fame. That means more than anything a literary critic could say.")

In a 1931 story called "The Aurelian"—an archaic term for butterfly collector—Nabokov describes a butterfly shop in Berlin whose windows are full of "eyed wings wide-open in wonder, shimmering blue satin, black magic." To the left of the shop there are stores that sell soap, coal, and bread; to the right, a tobacconist, a delicatessen, and a fruit seller. This is how Nabokov viewed butterflies. One may progress through life surrounded on all sides by drabness, but if there are butterflies at the center, there will never be a want of beauty or romance. What more appropriate passion could a writer have? Lepidopterists, more than naturalists of any other stripe, have long inclined toward the literary, as one can tell from looking at the names they have given the objects of their study. There are butterflies named after Homer, Catullus, Martial, Juvenal, Propertius, and Persius; after dozens of characters in Greek and Roman mythology; and even after punctuation marks—the question mark, the long dash, and the comma. (Nabokov described the comma in a famous passage about listening to his governess read French classics on the veranda of the family estate outside St. Petersburg, while his attention was joyfully diverted by the comma-like markings on a butterfly that had settled on the threshold.)

Nabokov began the sixth chapter of *Speak, Memory* —the greatest essay on butterfly collecting ever written— by describing the first butterfly he wanted to catch (a swallowtail) and, in the last paragraph, wrote:

> [T]he highest enjoyment of timelessness—in a landscape selected at random—is when I stand among rare butterflies and their food plants. This is ecstasy, and behind the ecstasy is something else, which is hard to explain. It is like a momentary vacuum into which rushes all that I love.

(My four favorite words in this passage are "and their food plants." Only a true entomologist, as opposed to a starry-eyed amateur, would include them in such a lyrical effusion and, what's more, clearly believe they were lyrical themselves.) Many of the themes in Nabokov's fiction—metamorphosis and flight, deception and mimicry, evasion and capture—are lepidopteran. And to my ear, his very language is too. The first canto of *Pale Fire* contains, within its four-and-a-half-page compass, the words *torquated, stillicide, shagbark, vermiculated, preterist, iridule*, and *lemniscate*. Nabokov collected rare words, just as he collected rare butterflies, and when he netted one, especially in the exotic landscape of his second language, his satisfaction is as palpable as if he had finally captured the brown and white hairstreak that once eluded him when he was a boy. Nabokov's style is not just poetic; it is taxonomic. He mentions with something close to hatred the village schoolmaster who, taking his charges for a nature walk, used to quash young Vladimir's hunger for precision by saying, "Oh, just a small bird—no special name." And what scorn Nabokov bears for *us*, his clueless audience, when he writes, "I had found last spring a dark aberration of Sievers' Carmelite (just another gray moth to the reader)."

Phase Two of my life as a collector—again, one shared with my older and wiser brother—was an intemperate, catholic, and nonmurderous surrender to the urge to identify the small bird and the gray moth. If catching was the central theme of our childhood, curating—classifying, labeling, sorting, arranging, displaying—was the central theme of our adolescence. Butterflies were the slender wedge that opened up something much larger: an earnest attempt to stuff the entire natural world, down to the last kingdom, phylum, class, order, family, genus, and species (I can still rattle these off in the proper sequence, having learned the mnemonic "King Philip, Come Out For God's Sake" at age twelve), into our spare bedroom. It never occurred to us that it would not fit.

The spare bedroom, on the southwest corner of the second floor of our house in Los Angeles, to which we had moved when I was eight and Kim was ten, had a sign on the door that read:

THE SERENDIPITY MUSEUM OF NATURE

NO SMOKING, PLEASE

The sign was embossed in blue with a Dymo Label-maker, than which there was no more perfect gift, circa 1963, for a pair of children who were crazy about naming things. I am not quite sure why our parents turned over this room to us, nor why they let us hammer pieces of whale baleen into the striped tan wallpaper, nor why they permitted us to fill the bathroom with dirt in order to accommodate our pet California king snake. All I can say is that I am profoundly grateful that they did.

In *Our Mutual Friend*, Silas Wegg visits a shop belonging to "Mr. Venus, Preserver of Animals and Birds, Articulator of human bones." Mr. Wegg is there because—could anyone but Dickens ever come up with this one?—he wishes to retrieve his leg, which Mr. Venus purchased, for potential inclusion in a skeleton, from the hospital in which it was amputated. "I shouldn't like," says Mr. Wegg, "to be what I may call dispersed, a part of me here, and a part of me there, but should wish to collect myself as a genteel person." (Mr. Wegg may thus be the only collector who has ever collected himself. He does get his leg back, though not until later in the book; it arrives under Mr. Venus's arm, carefully wrapped, look-

ing like "a sort of brown paper truncheon.") Mr. Venus
shows Mr. Wegg around the shop. "Bones, warious," he
explains.

> Skulls, warious. Preserved Indian baby. African ditto. Bot-
> tled preparations, warious. Everything within reach of your
> hand, in good preservation. The mouldy ones a-top. What's
> in those hampers over them again, I don't quite remember.
> Say, human warious. Cats. Articulated English baby. Dogs.
> Ducks. Glass eyes, warious. Mummied bird. Dried cuticle,
> warious. Oh, dear me! That's the general panoramic view.

The general panoramic view of the Serendipity Museum of Nature was similarly warious. It bore a far closer
resemblance to Mr. Venus's shop, or to a seventeenth-
century *Wunderkammer* crammed from top to bottom
with miscellaneous natural curiosities, than it did to any
museum we had actually seen.

We displayed not only things that had once been alive
but things that had once contained life: the discarded
skin of a garter snake, the exoskeleton of a cicada, the
speckled egg of a scrub jay, the pendant nest of a Balti-
more oriole. Blowfish dangled from the ceiling on strands
of dental floss. In the southeast corner, pinned to the
wall, were scraps of fur—leopard, tiger, polar bear, rab-
bit, otter, nutria, mink—left over from coats tailored by a
local furrier. Next to them was a man-size piece of Styro-
foam into which we had stuck hundreds of feathers. On
the west wall we had nailed a desiccated sand shark,
which looked like a crucified demon. Shelves and card tables held, among other things, a stuffed mouse, a stuffed

bat, the skeleton of a pit viper, a hornet's nest, a mounted ostrich egg, a hunk of petrified wood, the fossils of ammonites and foraminifers, several dried salamanders, a dead tarantula, three dead scorpions, a sperm-whale tooth, a box of our own baby teeth, the foot of an egret, a pickled squid, a pickled baby octopus, and a pickled human tapeworm, about which I am said to have exclaimed, when I received it on my tenth birthday, "Just what I always wanted!" There were also about a dozen bird and mammal skulls that we had retrieved from road kills and cleaned with bleach. (Pending their Clorox baths, our mother permitted us to wrap the corpses in aluminum foil and store them in the freezer, as long as we labeled them clearly enough to prevent her from confusing them with dinner.)

Our old Riker mounts hung on the south wall, but the black and yellow stripes of the tiger swallowtails were fading. Our new passion was shells, which we housed in a huge metal cabinet, typing the genera on little slips of paper and gluing them to the drawer fronts. In conchology, as a mid-nineteenth-century British magazine observed, "there is no cruelty in the pursuit, the subjects are so ornamental to a boudoir." It is true that on the Florida island where we spent our spring vacations, we did occasionally collect live king's crown conchs, boil them, extract the animals, and clean the shells with muriatic acid. (Being trusted with dangerous substances was a continuing theme throughout our childhood.) But it was more sporting, and more fun, to walk along the beach and, among the jetsam of broken cockles and clams, to spot a banded tulip, an alphabet cone, an apple murex, or (great find of my youth!) an angulate wentletrap.

Last week I was reminiscing about our museum with my brother. Kim said, "When you collect nature, there are two moments of discovery. The first comes when you find the thing. The second comes when you find the name." Few pleasures can equal those of the long summer afternoons we spent sitting on the floor in a patch of sunlight, our shell guides spread out before us, trying to identify a particular species of limpet or marginella—and finally, with a whoop of delight, succeeding. Without classification, a collection is just a hodgepodge. Taxonomy, after all—and I think we unconsciously realized this, even as teenagers—is a form of imperialism. During the nineteenth century, when British naval surveys were flooding London with specimens to be classified, inserting them into their proper niches in the Linnaean hierarchy had undeniable political overtones. Take a bird or a lizard or a flower from Patagonia or the South Seas, perhaps one that has had a local name for centuries, rechristen it with a Latin binomial, and presto! It has become a tiny British colony. That's how Kim and I felt, too. To name was to assert dominion.

"You're like a miser," Miranda says to her captor in *The Collector*. "You hoard up all the beauty in these drawers. . . . I hate people who collect things, and classify things and give them names." That's the popular notion, all right. Even my husband finds it a wee bit pathological when he finds me taking the shells *he* has collected and arranging them in rows, by species. But I believe it is no accident that the three greatest biological theorists of the nineteenth century—Alfred Russel Wallace; Henry Walter Bates, who developed the theory of mimicry; and Charles Darwin—were all, at their cores, collectors. Wallace, who collected plants as a boy, returned from the Malay Archipelago with 125,660 "specimens of natural history," mostly insects. Bates, who collected bugs as a boy, returned from the Amazon with 14,712 different *species*, again mostly insects, of which eight thousand were previously undiscovered. When he was a boy, Darwin collected coins, postal franks, pebbles, minerals, shells, birds' eggs, and, above all, in the days when "to beetle" was an infinitive, hundreds of specimens of the order Coleoptera. His zeal was such that once, with a rare beetle in each hand, he spied a third species, and popped the beetle in his right hand into his mouth. (Unfortunately, it ejected a foul-tasting liquid and he had to spit it out.) He later sent home from South America box after box of specimens—birds, mammals, reptiles, insects, fish—that he had skinned and stuffed and pickled while fighting terrible seasickness in the *Beagle*'s poop cabin. It was not enough just to *see* the Galápagos finches; he had to *collect* them, and get help classifying them, and compare their beaks back home in England, before he was able to develop the theory of the origin of species.

All nature collectors share a particular set of tastes and skills: pattern recognition; the ability to distinguish anomaly from norm; the compulsion to order experience.

A few of them also have brilliant imaginations, as well as what Darwin called the capacity for "grinding general laws out of large collections of facts." *Collections* of facts. Those of us who lack the latter two abilities will never change the course of science, but when we invite a new shell or butterfly into our lives, we are doing a part of what Darwin did. And lest the primacy of the collecting instinct be underestimated, let us reflect that Darwin was never able to remember for more than a few days a single date or a line of poetry, but at age sixty-seven, looking back on the beetles of his youth, he wrote, "I can remember the exact appearance of certain posts, old trees and banks where I made a good capture."

We sold the Serendipity Museum of Nature. My brother and I were off to college, our parents were moving to a smaller house, we thought it was time to grow up, and . . . well, we just did it. We put an ad in the *Los Angeles Times*, and over the course of a weekend, a stream of strange people walked underneath the blowfish and took away the field guides and the fossil ammonites and the desiccated sand shark and the pickled human tapeworm. The things we prized most, because we had found them ourselves, were worthless. I remember jamming dozens of birds' nests into plastic garbage bags. I was almost seventeen; it was the last day of my childhood.

Thank heavens, we kept the shells, because they were

small and easily stored. Today they rest inside a glass-fronted cabinet in the home of our elderly parents, who surprised us a few years ago by moving to the Florida island where we had collected the shells in the first place. When I visit, I still cannot resist picking up the odd murex or limpet when I walk along the beach. They do not have the same meaning they once did, but, as Swann said in *Remembrance of Things Past*, "even when one is no longer attached to things, it's still something to have been attached to them."

Three years ago, I found a 1951 edition of *A Field Guide to the Butterflies of North America, East of the Great Plains*, by Alexander B. Klots, in a secondhand store in upstate New York. There was a stamp on the school library bookplate that said DISCARDED. Discard *Klots*? How could anyone do that? I suppose for the same reason that I once discarded Klots myself: because there wasn't room. When I was younger, I didn't know what I wanted from life, so I wanted everything—new experiences, tiger swallowtails, egrets' feet. Now that I have collected a family, a home, a vocation, and a few thousand books, my New York City apartment and my life are full. Before my husband's last birthday, I sent for a copy of the Carolina Biological Supply Company catalog so I could buy him a flower press. I felt the old thirst when I read about the tarantula spiderling kit, $49.95; the owl pellets, "fumigated and individually wrapped," $3.20; the live salamander larvae, $11.45 a dozen; the slime mold box, "preferred by professional slime mold collectors" (a lovely phrase; I had never thought of it as a profession),

$5.80. I knew, however, that I would never order these things. There isn't room.

My favorite Nabokov story, "Christmas," is about a man named Sleptsov who has recently lost his son, a butterfly collector. In an agony of suicidal grief, Sleptsov looks through his son's belongings—spreading boards, specimen files, a net that still smells of summer and sun-warmed grass. Suddenly, from the biscuit tin in which it had been stored, the dormant cocoon of a great *Attacus* moth, stirred into life by the unaccustomed heat, bursts open. A wrinkled black creature the size of a mouse crawls out and slowly unfurls its wings. As soon as he witnesses this miracle, Sleptsov knows he must stay alive. "Christmas" is a story about lepidoptery, but it is also a story about parenthood. One reason we have children, I think, is to experience through them the miracle of the *Attacus* moth: to learn that parts of ourselves we had given up for dead are merely dormant, and that the old joys can re-emerge, fresh and new and in a completely different form.

I have two children. Henry, who is three, owns three rubber caterpillars—a black swallowtail, a pipevine swallowtail, and a zebra heliconian. I know their species because he likes to match them up with the pictures in Klots, which now sits on a shelf in his bedroom. Henry is at an age when anything seems possible, and the other night, having just looked at a diagram of metamorphosis, he saw a housefly crawling across the ceiling and said, with dreamy excitement, "Maybe that fly will turn into a stag beetle!"

Susannah is eight. When she was six, we gave her a kit containing five painted lady caterpillars. She watched them pupate. After they broke out of their chrysalises as fully formed butterflies, she carried them in a net enclosure from our cramped apartment to a nearby garden. Then she loosened the net and let them go.

THE UNFUZZY LAMB

His name is surely part of the problem. Had he been Charles Tiger, he might not have to drag behind him, like a tattered baby blanket, his undeserved reputation for being namby-pamby and fuddy-duddy. *He* didn't think he was lamblike. After his best friend, Samuel Taylor Coleridge, referred to him as "my gentle hearted Charles" in the 1797 poem "This Lime-Tree Bower My Prison," Lamb wrote him:

> In the next edition . . . please to blot out *gentle hearted*, and substitute drunken dog, ragged head, seld-shaven, odd-eye'd, stuttering, or any other epithet which truly and properly belongs to the Gentleman in question.

When I first read that letter, I misinterpreted it as polite self-deprecation: *Your poem is too kind; I do not merit such praise.* Now I recognize in Lamb's voice the same authentically aggrieved tone with which my three-year-old son casts off the constringent mantle of virtue: *Don't call me a good boy!*

Let me confess at the outset that I have a monumental crush on Charles Lamb. My fantasies are not precisely adulterous, but neither are they devoid of sensuality. Though never married and probably celibate, Lamb knew how to seize eros by the throat, give it a few sublimational shakes, and transform it into some of the most voluptuous prose ever written. In my mind's eye, we walk his beloved London streets ("O! her lamps of a night! her rich goldsmiths, printshops, toyshops, mercers, hardware-men, pastry-cooks! St. Paul's Churchyard! the Strand! Exeter Change! Charing Cross!"), stopping for a quick codfish dinner ("that manly firmness, combined with a sort of womanish coming-in-pieces") and then a book-stall browse ("venturing tenderly, page after page, expecting every moment when [the owner] shall interpose his interdict, and yet unable to deny [our]selves the gratification"), while he—small-bodied, large-headed, skinny-legged, tailcoated, top-hatted—recounts to me, with the characteristic stammer that only tobacco could loosen, an evening's worth of my favorite tales from *The Essays of Elia*.

I do not understand why so few other readers are clamoring for his company. It is a bad sign when a writer can be found more easily in secondhand bookstores—which, as I need hardly point out, are filled with books that people have gotten rid of—than in Barnes & Noble. I own seventeen volumes by and about Lamb, most of them out of print and, despite their engraved frontispieces and deckle-edged pages and grosgrain bookmarks, all of them ignominiously cheap. In England, the

Charles Lamb Society still toasts "The Immortal Memory" at dinners held annually to commemorate his birthday (February 10, 1775). But in the United States, where he was once more widely read than in his own country, Lamb is kept alive largely through the tenuous resuscitations of university English departments: the ICUs of literature.

I cannot say I loved him the instant I laid eyes on him. Like many people, I encountered *Tales from Shakespeare* (coauthored with Mary Lamb, who I assumed was his wife) at age ten or thereabouts, and thought it a snore. In high school, "A Dissertation upon Roast Pig" was served up as a model of the essay form, but I was of the age that hungers for descriptions of madness and violence, not of "crisp, tawny, well-watched, not overroasted, *crackling*." Then, in my late twenties, I read "Readers Against the Grain":

> Rather than follow in the train of this insatiable monster of modern reading, I would forswear my spectacles, play at put, mend pens, kill fleas, stand on one leg, shell peas, or do whatsoever ignoble diversion you shall put me to. Alas! I am hurried on in the vortex. I die of new books, or the everlasting talk about them . . . . I will go and relieve myself with a page of honest John Bunyan, or Tom Brown. Tom anybody will do, so long as they are not of this whiffling century.

I suppose my own century seemed pretty whiffling too, and in a mood of reactionary nostalgia—and also because I found the essay hilarious and lovely—I decided

that anyone who used the word *whiffling* deserved further investigation. A biographical note on Lamb referred,
as if it were common knowledge, to "the family tragedy."
What family tragedy? I looked it up. Ah. There was the
central event of Lamb's life, the hideous irritant around
which the nacre of his genius coalesced, the staggering
evidence that the dissertator on pork and pea-shelling
was in fact (if only I had known this at sixteen!) no
stranger to madness and violence. In 1796, when Lamb
was twenty-one, his sister lost her mind and murdered
their mother.

I could hardly believe it. *Lamb?* I did not yet know his
work—did not know how weird and dark it was, did not
know of the screeds on drunkenness and lost love and bad
dreams. I had no idea what his friend William Hazlitt
meant when he said, "His jests scald like tears." I was
stuck in the "gentle-hearted Charles" rut and could not
reconcile the passages I had read, all surface-skating,
with any intimate knowledge of "mangling, choking, stifling, scorching demons."

Now I know that he and those demons, which he described in an essay called "Witches and Other Night
Fears," were on familiar terms throughout his life. His
earliest memories were of nocturnal visitations from
hobgoblins, incubi, Chimeras, and Harpies. He insisted—
a century before Jung—that these apparitions were not
planted in his consciousness by scary stories, but already
resident: "The archetypes are in us, and eternal." I feel

certain, from two painfully recollective sentences he wrote in his forties, that his mother did not comfort him:

> Parents do not know what they do when they leave tender babes alone to go to sleep in the dark. The feeling about for a friendly arm—the hoping for a familiar voice—when they wake screaming—and find none to soothe them—what a terrible shaking it is to their poor nerves!

The son of an impoverished scrivener, Lamb was the last of seven children, four of whom died in infancy. His mother favored her more conventional elder son, John. Charles was raised largely by his sister, Mary, ten years his senior, who taught him the alphabet before he could speak and shared with him her fondness for *Pilgrim's Progress* and Foxe's *Book of Martyrs*. Mary was plain, bookish, and shy: like Charles, a mystery to their mother, who, he later observed, "*never understood* her right. She loved her, as she loved us all with a Mother's love, but in opinion, in feeling, & sentiment, & disposition, bore so distant a resemblance to her daughter, that she never understood her right." But Charles understood Mary, and she him, with an empathy so fine-tuned that she once burst into tears because she had (accurately) detected a tone of false cheer in his voice. "She is all his Comfort—he her's," Coleridge wrote Robert Southey when Lamb was in his late teens. Theirs was to be one of the strangest, strongest, and most inextricably entwined sibling relationships in history.

When Lamb was seven, he was packed off as a charity pupil to Christ's Hospital, a school founded in 1552 "to take out of the streets all the fatherless and other poor men's children that were not able to keep them." The best among the Christ's Hospital "Bluecoat Boys" received an incomparable education in English and Latin, accompanied by regular whacks on the palm with a ferule, occasional whippings with a scourge, and, if they attempted to run away, imprisonment in "little, square, Bedlam cells, where a boy could just lie at his length upon straw and a blanket . . . out of the reach of any sound, to suffer whatever horrors the weak nerves, and superstition incident to his time of life, might subject him to." Lamb feared the school, but he also loved it, not so much for its masters as for its students. "The Christ's Hospital boy's friends at school," he was to write, "are commonly his intimates through life."

That was assuredly true for him. For it was there that he met Coleridge, of whom he was to say, on his old schoolmate's death in 1834, "He was my fifty years old friend without a dissension." (Well, almost. They had a spat or two but never a permanent rift.) When they met, Lamb was seven and Coleridge nine: two homesick little boys who instantly recognized in each other an affinitive amalgam of intelligence, imagination, oddity, and misery. Though Coleridge's family stood higher on the social ladder—his father, who had died the year before Coleridge met Lamb, was a vicar—there were some remarkable congruences. Both were the youngest children in their families; both were misunderstood and ignored by their mothers; neither had a brother to whom he was close. (Coleridge would later describe his brothers as

"good men as times go—very good men; but alas! we
have neither Tastes or Feelings in common.") To the
beloved sister he had in Mary, Lamb added the beloved
brother—as he put it, "more than a brother!"—he found
in Coleridge.

When one looks back on the pair of them—Lamb
small and delicate, Coleridge tall and commanding—it
would seem at first glance that Coleridge had all the luck.
Coleridge went up to Cambridge; Lamb, despite a glori-
ous academic record, was forced to leave Christ's Hospital
at fourteen because of his stammer, which disqualified
him from the career of clergyman that all top Bluecoat
graduates were expected to pursue. Coleridge became a
poet and a radical; Lamb, while writing poetry on the
side, worked at a countinghouse and then, starting at seventeen, as a low-level clerk in the accountant's office of
the East India House. Coleridge married; Lamb did not.
Over the long run, however, the comparison becomes
muddier. Coleridge abandoned his wife and became an
opium addict; Lamb's life was, if nothing else (and
against all odds), stable.

Before that stability was achieved, however, Lamb
was ruled and nearly destroyed by demons. As we move
into the bitter heart of his life, there is a clear paper
trail for us to follow, for he recorded it all in a series of
letters to his "more than a brother." On May 27, 1796, he
wrote:

> My life has been somewhat diversified of late. The 6 weeks
> that finished last year & began this, your very humble ser-

vant spent very agreeably in a mad house at Hoxton. I am
got somewhat rational now, & don't bite anyone.

Insanity ran in the family, on his father's side, so Lamb
was not altogether surprised when overwork, financial
problems, and rejection by a fair-haired country girl
named Ann Simmons combined to bring on a "temporary frenzy." It also did not help that Coleridge, with
whom he had been meeting nightly in a local alehouse to
drink egghot and talk about metaphysics and poetry, had
recently decamped from London to Bristol. All we know
of the episode is that Lamb was indisputably irrational
("many a vagary my imagination played with me,
enough to make a volume if all told") and that the experience was not altogether unpleasant ("I had many many
hours of pure happiness. Dream not Coleridge, of having
tasted all the grandeur & wildness of Fancy, till you have
gone mad"). The self-mocking levity was characteristic,
as was the bizarrely incongruous postscript: "My civic
and poetic compliments to Southey if at Bristol. Why, he
is a very Leviathan of Bards!—the small minnow, I!"
Went mad. Oh, by the way, say hi to Robert.
Over the next four months, six long letters followed,
filled mostly with close and useful criticism of Coleridge's works in progress, but occasionally breaking into
paroxysms of loneliness:

Thank you for your frequent letters: you are the only corre-
spondent, and I might add, the only friend I have in the
world. I go nowhere, and have no acquaintance. Slow of

speech, and reserved of manners, no one seeks or cares for my society; and I am left alone.

Alone, that is, except for his family—invalid mother, senile father, elderly aunt, anxious sister—whose constant proximity, in their cramped lodgings on Little Queen Street, must have seemed more suffocation than comfort. Mary, who for several years had had periods of prostrating depression, supplemented her brother's clerking salary with long hours of needlework and also bore the brunt of her mother's care, waiting on her during the day and sharing her restless bed at night.

On September 27, Lamb wrote Coleridge:

My dearest friend—

White or some of my friends or the public papers by this time may have informed you of the terrible calamities that have fallen on our family. I will only give you the outlines. My poor dear dearest sister in a fit of insanity has been the death of her own mother. I was at hand only time enough to snatch the knife out of her grasp. She is at present in a mad house, from whence I fear she must be moved to an hospital. God has preserved to me my senses,—I eat and drink and sleep, and have my judgment I believe very sound. My poor father was slightly wounded, and I am left to take care of him and my aunt . . . . Write,—as religious a letter as possible—but no mention of what is gone and done with.—With me "the former things are passed away," and I have something more to do than to feel. God Almighty have us all in His keeping.—

C. Lamb

Five days before he wrote those words, Lamb had arrived home from work to find his mother pierced to the
heart with a carving knife, his father wounded in the
head with a fork, and his sister still gripping the bloody
murder weapon. Mary had apparently become enraged at
her young dressmaking apprentice, picked up the knife,
and chased the girl around the dining room. Her mother
begged her to stop, the girl escaped, and Mary stabbed
her mother. A jury that was convened the next day
swiftly returned a verdict of lunacy.

I doubt that anyone has ever read this letter without
noticing the adjectives that Lamb lavished on his "poor
dear dearest sister" but withheld from his murdered
mother. Matricide has never inspired less sympathy for
the victim and more for the perpetrator. The letters that
Lamb poured out to Coleridge over the next month constitute a most peculiar psychological record. About Mary,
who was kindly tended by "the good Lady of the Mad
house, & her daughter . . . [who] love her & are taken
with her amazingly," he wrote:

> Of all the people I ever saw in the world, my poor sister was
> most and thoroughly devoid of the least tincture of selfish-
> ness. I will enlarge upon her qualities, poor dear, dearest
> soul, in a future letter, for my own comfort, for I understand
> her thoroughly; and if I mistake not, in the most trying sit-
> uation that a human being can be found in, she will be
> found—(I speak not with sufficient humility, I fear,) but,
> humanly and foolishly speaking, she will be found, I trust,
> uniformly great and amiable.

And:

> Within a day or two of the fatal one, we dressed for dinner
> a tongue, which we had had salted for some weeks in the
> house. As I sat down, a feeling like remorse struck me: this
> tongue poor Mary got for me; and can I partake of it now,
> when she is far away?

There were hundreds of words about missing Mary, and
not one about missing his mother. In fact, he mentioned
her at any length only twice: once when he found his way
"mechanically" (a horrifically honest adverb) to the side
of her coffin, where he begged her forgiveness for forget-
ting her so soon, and once, after angrily observing that
she had never appreciated her daughter, when he reminded himself, "Still she was a good mother, God forbid
I should think of her but *most* respectfully, *most* affec-
tionately." He was trying hard with those italics, but his
heart wasn't in it.

Lamb's older brother, John, who was "little disposed
(I speak not without tenderness for him) at any time to
take care of old age & infirmities," managed to wriggle
out of his familial responsibilities and dump them all on
twenty-one-year-old Charles. Lamb—who was, after all,
an accountant—calculated that his father's pension and
his own salary together produced about £180 a year, "out
of which we can spare £50 or £60 at least for Mary while
she stays at Islington [a private asylum] . . . . If my father,
an old servant maid, & I cant live & live comfortably on
£130 or £120 a year we ought to burn by slow fires, & I almost would, that Mary might not go into an hospital."

John thought Mary should be locked up in a mental institution, preferably Bedlam, for life; Charles was deter-
mined to take care of her himself. He bided his time for
two and a half years until his father, who he knew would
never accept Mary's homecoming, had the courtesy to
die. Ten days later, taking advantage of an act that allowed an insane criminal to be "liberated on security being given that he should properly be taken care of as a
lunatic," Lamb brought Mary home. As Sir Thomas
Noon Talfourd, Lamb's friend and first biographer, put it,
"he satisfied all the parties who had power to oppose her
release, by his solemn engagement that he would take
her under his care for life; and he kept his word."

Wordsworth, who himself lived with his sister, before
and during his marriage, for fifty-five years, wrote of the
Lambs:

> *Her love*
> *(What weakness prompts the voice to tell it here?)*
> *Was as the love of mothers; and when years,*
> *Lifting the boy to man's estate, had called*
> *The long protected to assume the part*
> *Of the protector, the first filial tie*
> *Was undissolved; and in or out of sight*
> *Remained imperatively interwoven*
> *With life itself.*

Charles and Mary shared a household for thirty-six years,
in a state of what Lamb called "double singleness." They
spent their evenings in front of the fire, Mary darning
socks while Charles read Elizabethan poetry aloud. They

wrote *Tales from Shakespeare* together, he taking the tragedies and she the comedies, working, as she described it, "on one table (but not on one cushion sitting), like Hermia and Helena in the Midsummer's Night's Dream; or, rather, like an old literary Darby and Joan." A collection of his sonnets was

WITH ALL A BROTHER'S FONDNESS,
INSCRIBED TO
MARY ANN LAMB,
THE AUTHOR'S BEST FRIEND AND SISTER.

They visited France together ("I & sister are just returned from Paris!! We have eaten frogs"). When he was forty-eight and she was fifty-eight, they affirmed their coupledom by adopting a teenage orphan girl, who later married Lamb's publisher.

Mary was lucid and even-tempered most of the time, but under stress—a servant's death, a change of lodging—she often relapsed into insanity, and Lamb would walk her, weeping, to Hoxton Asylum, carrying a straitjacket. "What sad large pieces it cuts out of life," he wrote during one such absence. During another, his despair overflowed to Coleridge in the blackest letter of his life:

> Mary will get better again; but her constantly being liable to such relapses is dreadful,—nor is it the least of our Evils, that her case & all our story is so well known around us. We are in a manner *marked* . . . . I am completely shipwreck'd—My head is quite bad. I almost wish that Mary were dead.

It pains me to say it, but I feel quite sure that if Mary had not murdered her mother, her brother would never have become Elia, the persona he assumed in the great essays he wrote in his late forties. I also feel quite sure that Elia would never have been born if Lamb had not been compelled to work as a clerk.

For thirty-three years, Lamb sat on a high stool, identical to those occupied by thirty other clerks; dipped his goose quill into two inkwells, one containing black ink and the other red (he called the latter Clerk's Blood); and recorded the prices of tea, indigo, and piece goods. Not only did he hate his work; as Winifred F. Courtney, one of the most perceptive of his biographers, has pointed out, he was *bad* at it. Courtney examined some of Lamb's ledgers and found that he frequently made mistakes. He rubbed them out with his little finger, but they nonetheless haunted his dreams, from which, he wrote in one of his Elia essays, he "would awake with terrors of imaginary false entries." It is worth remembering that while he was adding up figures in the East India House's stygian offices at Nos. 12–21 Leadenhall Street (what name could be more appropriate?), his friends—Coleridge, Southey, Wordsworth, Godwin, De Quincey— were rambling in the Lake Country, experimenting with mind-altering drugs, siring illegitimate children, and planning a utopian community in America ("We shall . . . criticise poetry when hunting a buffalo," wrote Southey). And yet, improbable as it seems, Lamb was an essential member of their coterie. It's as if the inner circle of the Beats had consisted of Kerouac, Ginsberg,

Corso, Burroughs, Ferlinghetti, and an accountant at H&R Block.

When I first read Lamb, I imagined his life as an essayist to have been a pleasant stroll along a level, well-trod path. Now I see it as a technical climb along a knife-edged ridge, with a thousand-foot drop on either side. To the left lay the memory of the "day of horrors" and the constant anxiety over Mary's sanity, both of which threatened his own sanity as well as his ability to summon up sufficient calm to write. To the right lay the deadening drudgery of Leadenhall, which threatened to swallow his creativity whole. (Remember that during Melville's nineteen years as a customs inspector, he wrote absolutely nothing of note.) In the narrow space between anarchy and regimentation lay his essays, which I believe were made possible by—and also protected him from—his life's opposed poles.

Before the murder, Lamb had published only poems, and they were uniformly terrible. Immediately afterward, he told Coleridge: "Mention nothing of poetry. I have destroyed every vestige of past vanities of that kind." The intended renunciation did not last long, but the output lessened, and, with a couple of exceptions, the quality did not improve. Because he took poetry far more seriously than prose, after the murder it seemed a self-indulgence, a "vanity"—unlike journalism, which paid, and thus contributed to Mary's keep. In the dedication to Coleridge that introduced his *Collected Works* of 1818, he wrote, "The sap (if ever it had any) has become, in a manner, dried up and extinct: and you will find your old associate . . . dwindled into prose and *criticism.*"

The "dwindling" was, in fact, a miraculous expansion. When he wrote those self-effacing words, he had already published some fine literary and theatrical criticism, but he was to find his true voice in the fifty-two essays—on chimney sweeps, on weddings, on old books, on sickness, on gallantry, on witches, on beggars, on roast pig, on ears—that he wrote between 1820 and 1825, working nights and Sundays, for the *London Magazine.* "True voice" is an odd phrase to use for a series of works written under a pseudonym (he borrowed "Elia" from an Italian clerk who had worked with his brother) and, though autobiographical, mendacious in some crucial respects. Elia, for instance, wrote, "Brother, or sister, I never had any—to know them. A sister, I think, that should have been Elizabeth, died in both our infancies." Mary became the more comfortably distant "cousin Bridget," who was, of course, neither insane nor a murderess. Lamb's mother was never mentioned; his father was transmuted into an amiable factotum named Lovel, no relation to Elia. And while the real Lamb cared devotedly for his relatives, Elia called *his* poor relations "a lion in your path,—a frog in your chamber,—a fly in your ointment,—a mote in your eye." By such therapeutic subterfuges did Lamb's imagination extricate him from his family's stifling bonds.

True voice it was: funny (unlike Lamb the poet), intimate (unlike Lamb the accountant), and relaxed (unlike

Lamb the family pillar). But not inextinguishable. On March 29, 1825, Lamb retired, with a generous pension, from the East India House, an event he chronicled in "The Superannuated Man." This was Coleridge's favorite essay; he called it "worthy of Charles Lamb in his happiest Carolo-lambian Hour." With heartbreaking bafflement, the superannuated Elia, released from the "thraldom" of his own clerkship, confessed, "I wandered about thinking I was happy, and knowing I was not . . . . I missed my old chains, forsooth, as if they had been some necessary part of my apparel." Lamb lived nine more years but wrote no more great essays. He and Elia had retired together, and without the clerk's humble vantage point, he found himself without a platform. Just as Lamb had required Mary's madness to nudge him from poetry to prose, so he required his old chains to liberate the unpretentious alter ego who defined the modern familiar essay.

Lamb once compared bad journalists to "the *crooked man*, of whom a facetious Greek Professor relates this comical story, that he swallowed a *tenpenny nail*, and voided it out a cork-screw!" Lamb did the opposite: he swallowed a series of corkscrews and turned them into tenpenny nails. I have spent many a Carolo-lambian Hour grieving over his life's unfair twists and turns and wishing that posterity could vindicate Elia's efforts to straighten them out. "Damn the age!" Lamb once said. "I will write for antiquity." Antiquity is not cooperating. My dog-eared 1933 anthology (the dog-eared part is fine; Lamb preferred well-thumbed volumes), called

Everybody's Lamb, has become Hardly Anybody's Lamb. If I could make him Everybody's again, in my own whiffling century, I would forswear my spectacles, play at put, mend pens, kill fleas, stand on one leg, or shell peas.

ICE CREAM

I read last March that the town council of Stafford, New Jersey, had passed an ordinance stating: "At no time shall a vendor be permitted to use a sound device, mechanical bell, mechanical music, mechanical noise, speakers, [or] amplifiers." The target was ice cream trucks, whose peripatetic tootles the council wished to classify with the roar of jets and the blast of car alarms. As a child in suburban Connecticut, I had always considered the purl of the Good Humor truck to be more closely akin to a cricket's chirp or the sound of summer rain: a seasonal gift, wreathed in sweet associations. I was therefore heartened to read, in May, that Jeffery Cabaniss, the owner of Jef-Freeze Treats, had successfully challenged the constitutionality of Stafford's anti-tootle law in federal court. Mr. Cabaniss's only concession was to change his truck's melody from "Turkey in the Straw," which had particularly vexed the residents of Stafford, to the less familiar, and thus presumably less irksome, "Music Box Dancer."

The New York Times called Mr. Cabaniss a "First Amendment hero." I didn't give a fig about the Constitution. I cared about the contents of Mr. Cabaniss's truck. As far as I was concerned, a vote against Jef-Freeze Treats was a vote against ice cream, and a vote against ice cream—even against Klondike Krunch Bars and Power Ranger Pops, which constitute the heart of the Cabaniss inventory—was a vote against the pursuit of happiness.

I recently calculated (assuming an average consumption of one pint of ice cream per week, at 1,000 calories per pint, and the American Medical Association's reckoning of 3,500 calories per pound of stored body fat) that had I eaten no ice cream since the age of eighteen, I would currently weigh −416 pounds. I might be lighter than air, but I would be miserable. Before I was married, I frequently took a pint of Häagen-Dazs Chocolate Chocolate Chip to bed, with four layers of paper towels wrapped around the container to prevent digital hypothermia. (The Nutrition Facts on the side of the carton define a "serving size" as a quarter of a pint, but that's like calling a serving size of Pringles a single potato chip.) Now, under the watchful eye of a husband so virtuous that he actually prefers low-fat frozen yogurt, I go through the motions of scooping a modest hemisphere of ice cream into a small bowl, but we both know that during the course of the evening I will simply shuttle to and from the freezer until the entirety of the pint has been transferred from carton to bowl to me. A major incentive for writing this essay was that during its composition this process was not called greed; it was called research.

My favorite flavors are all variations on chocolate, vanilla, coffee, and nuts, none of which is good for you. I do not like fruit flavors. They are insufficiently redolent of sin. Strawberry ripple is the top of a slippery slope at the bottom of which lie such nouvelle atrocities, recently praised in *The New York Times*, as tofu-anise, cardamom, white pepper, and corn ice creams. *Corn?* Why not Brussels sprouts? (I shouldn't say that too loudly, lest the Ohio State University Department of Dairy Technology, which has created sauerkraut sherbet and potatoes-and-bacon ice cream, derive inspiration for a new recipe.) On the other hand, ice cream shouldn't actually kill you. When I called the Häagen-Dazs Consumer Relations Department a few days ago to verify the butterfat content of Mint Chip, I was alarmed to hear the following after-hours message: "If you have a medical emergency with one of our products that requires immediate attention, please call Poison Control at 612-347-2101." What medical emergency could a few scoops of ice cream possibly precipitate? It is true that circa 400 B.C., Hippocrates, or one of the anonymous writers who were later known as Hippocrates, warned that snow-chilled beverages might "suddenly throw . . . the body into a different state than it was before, producing thereby many ill effects." It is also true that in 1997 the *British Medical Journal* noted that "ice cream headaches" can be produced by cold temperatures on the back of the palate, which stimulate the spheno-palatine ganglion to dilate blood vessels in the brain. However, the article concluded with the heartening sentence "Ice cream abstinence is not indicated."

As I have said, I take a dim view of healthful ice cream, and was thus cheered to learn from a spokeswoman at the International Dairy Foods Association that sales of high-fat ice cream are going up and sales of low-fat ice cream are going down. Had I lived in eighteenth-century Naples, however, I might have softened my anti-salubrity stance. According to Filippo Baldini, a physician who wrote a 1775 treatise on the medicinal properties of *sorbetti*, cinnamon ices are an efficacious remedy for diarrhea; coffee ices for indigestion; pine-nut ices for consumption; ass's-milk ices for maladies of the blood; cow's-milk ices for paralysis; and sheep's-milk ices for hemorrhages, scurvy, and emaciation. This pharmacopoeia sounds right up my alley. In fact, if Dr. Baldini were practicing today, I would add my name to his patient rolls without delay. "You're looking a trifle emaciated, Ms. Fadiman," he'd say. "Here's a prescription for Ben & Jerry's New York Super Fudge Chunk. BlueCross BlueShield will reimburse in full."

Although very cold ice cream numbs the taste buds that perceive sweetness (the basis for the entreaty that used to adorn cartons of Häagen-Dazs: "Please temper to a soft consistency to achieve the full flavor bouquet"), I prefer my ice cream untempered. I also like it even better in the winter than in the summer. Seasonal Good Humor trucks notwithstanding, it is a grave error to assume that ice cream consumption requires hot weather. If that were the case, wouldn't Ben Cohen and Jerry Greenfield have established their first ice cream parlor in Tallahassee instead of Burlington, Vermont, which averages 161 annual days of frost? (Ben explains his product's winter popularity by means of the Internal-External Temperature Differential and Equalization Theory, whereby, he claims, the ingestion of cold foodstuffs in freezing weather reduces the difference between the internal body temperature and the ambient air temperature, thus making his customers feel comparatively warm.) Wouldn't John Goddard, an outdoorsman of my acquaintance, have arranged for a thermos of hot chicken soup instead of a half gallon of French vanilla ice cream with raspberry topping to be airdropped to him on the summit of Mount Rainier? And wouldn't the Nobel Prize banquet, held every year in Stockholm on the tenth of December, conclude with *crêpes Suzette* instead of *glace Nobel*? As the lights dim, a procession of uniformed servitors marches down the grand staircase, each bearing on a silver salver a large cake surrounded by spun sugar. Projecting from the cake is a dome of ice cream. Projecting from the dome is an obelisk of ice cream. Projecting from the obelisk is a flame. When the laureates—who have already consumed the likes of *homard en gelée à la crème de choux fleur et au caviar de Kalix* and *ballotine de pintade avec sa garniture de pommes de terre de Laponie* with no special fanfare—see what is heading their way, they invariably burst into applause.

The Greek grammarian Athenaeus tells a catty story about Diphilus, an Athenian dramatist who lived in the fourth century B.C.:

Once upon a time Diphilus was invited to Gnathaena's house, to dine, so they say, in celebration of the festival of Aphrodite. . . . And one of her lovers, a stranger from Syria, had sent her some snow . . . the snow was to be secretly shaken up in the unmixed wine; then she directed the slave to pour out about a pint and offer the cup to Diphilus. Overjoyed, Diphilus quickly drank out of the cup, and overcome by the surprising effect he cried, "I swear, Athena and the gods bear me witness, Gnathaena, that your wine-cellar is indubitably cold." And she replied, "Yes, for we always take care to pour in the prologues of your plays."

When the prologues of Diphilus were unavailable, the ancient Greeks and Romans, who had borrowed the trick from the Middle East, sometimes chilled their drinks with ice and snow. The ice, which was cut in winter from ponds and streams, and the snow, which was carried from mountaintops, were stored underground in straw-lined pits. If the pits were sufficiently well insulated, their contents could remain frozen throughout the summer.

By the seventeenth century, rich Florentines were so addicted to cold drinks that, in a poem called "Bacco in Toscano," Francesco Redi called snow "the fifth element":

> He is mad who without snow
> Thinks to receive a satisfied guest.
> Bring then from Vallombrosa
> Snow in God's plenty. . . .
> And bring me ice
> From the grotto under the Boboli hill.

With long picks
With great poles
Shatter
crush
crunch
crack, chip
Until all resolves
In finest iciest powder . . .

Redi also mentioned something called *pappina*, a semi-solid dessert made from snow beaten with fruit juices or other flavorings. However, as the late British food writer Elizabeth David observed in *Harvest of the Cold Months: The Social History of Ice and Ices*, "Ice-diluted and ice-cooled sherbets do not . . . equate with frozen sherbets any more than putting a few pieces of ice into a glass of drinking water turns that water into ice, or than the milk half-frozen in the bottle on your doorstep on an icy morning has become ice-cream."

It has long been believed that *real* sherbets and ice creams—desserts that were artificially frozen by submerging their containers in icy brine or other refrigerants—were introduced to France in the sixteenth century by Catherine de Medici, the wife of Henry II, who brought the recipes from Italy. In 1861, Isabella Beeton, the author of a British domestic bible called *The Book of Household Management*, declared this contribution to French cuisine so invaluable that Catherine should be forgiven the Massacre of St. Bartholomew's Day. Elizabeth David pooh-poohs the Catherine story. *She* thinks the Italians did not figure out how to make ice cream until the seventeenth century and that the first French ices were made around 1660 by a distiller named Audiger. This is Audiger's recipe for strawberry *sorbet*:

> For [32 oz.] of water crush one pound of strawberries in the said water, add eight to ten ounces of sugar, and then the juice of a lemon. . . . When the sugar has melted, and all is well incorporated, filter the mixture through a sieve, and cool it. . . . Put three, four, or six containers or other vessels according to their size in a tub, at one finger's distance each from the other, then you take the ice, which you pound well, and salt it when it is pounded, and promptly put it in the tub all round your boxes. . . . When all is thus arranged you leave it for half an hour, or three quarters. . . . Then you move the ice covering your boxes and stir the liquor with a spoon so that it freezes into a snow.

During the eighteenth and nineteenth centuries, Italians were believed to make the best frozen desserts. (Many people still hold this opinion, including a friend of mine who, on a recent visit to Sicily, was told by some local friends that they wished him to experience a "traditional Catania breakfast." He had lugubrious visions of pasta heaped with eggplant. However, the breakfast, served at an elegant café, turned out to be *granita di caffé con panna*: an espresso-flavored quasi-sherbet topped with whipped cream.) In 1778, a Benedictine monk in Apulia published recipes for ices and ice creams flavored with coffee, chocolate, cinnamon, candied eggs, chestnuts, pistachios, almonds, fennel seeds, violets, jasmine, oranges, lemons, strawberries, peaches, pears, apricots, bitter cherries, melons, watermelons, pomegranates, and

muscatel grapes. In Victorian Britain, the duke of Beaufort employed a Neapolitan confectioner who invented a
new *sorbetto* (the flavor, unfortunately, is not recorded), a
feat so momentous that it warranted waking His Grace in
the middle of the night to tell him the good news.

On the other side of the Atlantic, the earliest record
of ice cream dates to 1744. The man who ate it, at the
home of the governor of Maryland, said it went down
"Deliciously." His tastes were shared by George Washington, who owned two pewter ice cream pots, and
Thomas Jefferson, who developed his own eighteen-step
recipe. It was not until after James Madison became president in 1809, however, that ice cream realized its full
ceremonial potential. A White House guest wrote:

> Mrs. Madison always entertains with Grace and Charm, but
> last night there was a sparkle in her eye that set astir an Air
> of Expectancy among her Guests. When finally the brilliant
> Assemblage—America's best—entered the dining room,
> they beheld a Table set with French china and English sil-
> ver, laden with good things to eat, and in the Centre high on
> a silver platter, a large, shining dome of pink Ice Cream.

After that historic moment, it seems inevitable that in
1921, the commissioner of Ellis Island would decree that
all newly arrived immigrants be served ice cream as part
of their first American meal.

Americans now eat more ice cream per capita than the
citizens of any other nation, and I am proud to say that

from an early age I have worked hard to do my part for my country. I fixed the starting date of my own ice cream calculus at age eighteen because that marked the beginning of the period when I could consume my favorite food ad libitum. However, a substantial fraction of my pre-adult self was also made up of cream, milk, sugar, egg yolks, vanilla extract, and carrageenan (a natural stabilizer made from *Chondrus crispus*, a cartilaginous red alga that is harvested with long rakes from intertidal rocks along the North Atlantic).

Although partial to Toasted Almond Good Humors, I was aware, even as a very young child, that the kingdom of ice cream contains an exquisite haut monde as well as an affable proletariat. On special occasions, my parents would arrive home from New York City bearing a lavender box, swathed in dry ice, from Louis Sherry, in which reposed a frozen confection called Mocha Praliné. (O vanished love! What would I not give for a taste of you now!) Shaped like a birthday cake, Mocha Praliné was made of coffee ice cream decorated with fluted extrusions of whipped cream (*frozen* whipped cream, which gently resisted the tooth rather than squishing) and embedded with Tootsie Roll–sized logs of hazelnut-impregnated chocolate fudge. The logs were faintly gritty in texture and—there is no other way to describe them—excremental in color and shape. Who knows what regressive satisfactions, what thrillingly broken taboos, were bound up in their consumption?

When I was in the third grade, we moved to Los Angeles, where Mocha Praliné was unavailable and my brother and I were consequently morose. Our mother, to her everlasting credit, attempted to console us by frequently taking us to lunch at Blum's. Lunch was a chocolate milkshake. Period. (Although on other occasions she touted the merits of raw carrots and whole wheat bread, she was wise enough to recognize that if you drank an entire milkshake—the contents of the soda glass *plus* the contents of the metal shaker—you would hardly touch your hamburger anyway, so why order one?) As teenagers, we favored bowls of Baskin-Robbins Chocolate Mint (the color of fly-specked absinthe), which we bought by the half gallon, carried home on our bicycles, and excavated with a spade large enough to dig a grave.

In the fall of 1974, en route from California to our college in Boston, Kim and I decided to conduct a transcontinental ice cream tasting. We plotted our zigzag journey on a huge map, basing our ports of call on the recommendations of friends, and, after we sampled each shop's wares, assigned them a rating ranging from one to three ice cream cones. Starting at McConnell's in Santa Barbara (three cones), we pressed on to Snelgrove in Salt Lake City (two cones); Platte Valley Creamery in Scottsbluff, Nebraska (two and a half cones); Snowbird Frozen Custard in Indianapolis (one and a half cones); Ohio State University Creamery in Columbus (one and a half cones); and Bailey's in Cambridge (two cones). As you can see, it was all downhill after McConnell's, the sanctum sanctorum of ice cream: a shrine so beneficent that it served two kinds of vanilla (with and without specks), two kinds of chocolate (milk and bittersweet), and two kinds of coffee (smooth and peppered with ground espresso beans, samples of which an undeserving customer once Scotch-taped to a letter that said, "WHAT THE HELL IS THIS STUFF IN MY ICE CREAM?").

Fifteen years later, when my husband and I got married, it was a foregone conclusion—at least on my part—that ice cream would play an important role in the ceremonies. At our rehearsal dinner, our New York City loft was filled with the strange grinding noises of three hand-crank ice cream makers, each of which, under Kim's supervision, produced five quarts: vanilla, coffee, and mint chip. George and I gave the other members of the wedding party engraved silver pens. Kim received an engraved silver ice cream scoop.

My brother and his scoop now reside in Jackson, Wyoming. Although Kim works as a mountaineering guide, leads kayak expeditions, plays jazz recorder, teaches courses on snow morphology and the aerodynamics of bird flight, takes nature photographs, and manages a small investment fund, I think of him primarily as Wyoming's Emperor of Ice Cream.

Every few months, under the auspices of Central Wyoming College, Kim offers a class on the physics and chemistry of ice cream making. Have you ever wondered why homemade ice cream requires a mixture of ice and salt between the tub and the canister? Answer: salt lowers the freezing point of water by pushing apart the crystal lattice of ice, drawing the energy needed for this disruption by stealing heat from the ice cream mix. If there was no salt packed around the canister to cool the melting ice below 32 degrees, the mix, which freezes at around 27 degrees, would remain liquid even if you cranked for a hundred years.

Aside from the ingredients, what are the two most important variables in ice cream production? Answer: butterfat, which should be high, and overrun, which should be low. Ice cream must legally have a butterfat content of least 10 percent. Ben & Jerry's has 15 percent; McConnell's has 17 percent (and formerly had 22 percent, but too many customers complained that, post-sundae, the roofs of their mouths felt waxy). Overrun is the proportion of air whipped into the mix while it freezes. The cheapest commercial ice cream, which has 100 percent overrun, is half air and has the consistency of frozen shaving cream; McConnell's has 15 percent overrun and the consistency of ambrosia. Kim likes to reduce the overrun of Breyers Coffee, which he rates excellent in flavor but excessively fluffy in texture, by placing a few scoops in a plastic bag and smashing them with a meat-tenderizing mallet. ("How often do you do this?" I asked. "Always!" he answered. "Why eat all that air when it's so easy to get it out?")

What makes the mix turn into a scoopable mush rather than a greasy ice cube? Answer: the combination of cold and agitation, which can be accomplished in a commercial ice cream freezer, an electric home ice cream maker, a hand-cranker, or the back of a B-17 bomber. According to a 1943 *New York Times* article Kim is fond of quoting, American airmen stationed in Britain "place prepared ice-cream mixture in a large can and anchor it to the rear gunner's compartment of a Flying Fortress. It is well shaken up and nicely frozen by flying over enemy territory at high altitudes."

Alternatively, you can use liquid nitrogen. Kim's ice-cream-making technique underwent a revolution a decade ago, after a geology expedition in Yellowstone with two friends—one the daughter of the *pâtissier* to the king of Denmark, the other a geochronologist from U.C. Berkeley. As they were climbing Dunraven Pass, Kim mentioned—somehow it seemed apropos—that he had never been able to make a perfect homemade ice cream because the mix took about half an hour to freeze, during which time its ice crystals grew, through the process of melt-freeze metamorphosis, to a larger than optimal size. The geochronologist, whose name was Garniss Curtis, commented that a colder refrigerant would freeze the mix faster.

"I've tried dry ice bubbling in alcohol," said Kim. "It was a mess."

"No," said Professor Curtis. "I mean *really* cold. Dry ice is only minus 107 Fahrenheit. Liquid nitrogen is minus 320."

Kim returned to Jackson and took a large thermos bottle to the local sperm bank, which uses liquid nitrogen to preserve its merchandise. "Young man," said the director, eyeing the thermos, "that's quite a contribution." Kim explained that he wished to make a withdrawal, not a deposit. He took home a liter of liquid nitrogen and became an instant convert.

In the brave new world of nitro, no ice cream maker, either hand-crank or electric, is necessary. If the mix has been pre-chilled in a kitchen freezer, liquid nitrogen freezes it so fast that one needs only a metal pot and a metal stirring spoon (glass or plastic would shatter). I have frequently witnessed the process, which can justly be described as Macbethian. Because liquid nitrogen boils at 320 degrees below zero, when it comes into contact with warm air and is forced to change from a liquid to a gas, it seethes and steams like water in a spaghetti pot.

Although Kim has created many more complex recipes, the following ultra-simple one is my favorite. I'm not sure you should try it at home.

KIM FADIMAN'S COFFEE KAHLÚA
LIQUID NITROGEN ICE CREAM

1. Mix one pint half-and-half and one pint heavy cream.
2. Stir in several teaspoons good instant coffee, to taste.
3. Stir in sugar to taste (at least one cup: remember that because cold desensitizes sweet-sensitive taste buds, frozen ice cream will taste less sweet than mix).
4. Stir in Kahlúa to taste (at least two tablespoons).
5. Chill mix in kitchen freezer for about forty minutes, until small ice crystals begin to form around periphery.
6. Pour one inch of mix into large metal kitchen pot with insulated handle.
7. Ask friend with steady hands and thick gloves to hold handle.
8. Put on goggles and gloves.
9. Slowly pour liquid nitrogen from Dewar flask into pot while stirring mix vigorously with metal spoon, continuously scraping freezing mix off interior of pot. Liquid nitrogen will freeze flesh as well as ice cream. Watch where you pour.

10. Resist temptation to pour in big slug all at once. This creates spectacular mushroom cloud but freezes ice cream to texture of fossilized Rice Krispies.
11. When mix is stiff but not brittle, stop pouring. Wait until bubbling and hissing stop. If you eat ice cream before liquid nitrogen turns to vapor, you will suffer frostbite of the throat.

Kim has never suffered frostbite of the throat, though he did once suffer frostbite of the toes when he splashed a few −320° drops on his bare feet. However, in defense of liquid nitrogen, he hastens to mention that his only ice cream near-fatality occurred in connection with an old-fashioned hand-cranker in his pre-nitro days.

He was on a river trip in the Grand Canyon. Because he was one of the organizers, he had been able to conceal in the food supplies, without the knowledge of the other paddlers, a five-quart ice cream maker, a large sack of rock salt, and an insulated picnic chest containing several bags of ice and the ingredients for coffee ice cream. On the fifth morning of the trip, with his tent neatly stuffed and his gear stowed, he found himself waiting impatiently on the riverbank for the other expedition members to get ready. After an hour, he threw the ice cream ingredients into his kayak, threaded the rope of his quick-release rescue rig through the drain hole of the ice cream maker, and set off down the Colorado River.

Paddling alone in the Grand Canyon is a bad idea. Paddling alone in the Grand Canyon with a five-quart ice cream maker strapped to the back deck of your kayak is a *very* bad idea. In the middle of Nankoweap Rapid, a wave broke over the stern, filled the tub of the ice cream maker, and tipped Kim over. Normally, he would easily have performed an Eskimo roll, a way of bracing the paddle against the water in order to turn an upside-down kayak right side up. However, the weight and drag of the water-filled tub created so much resistance that he was unable to roll.

Zooming through the rapid upside down, his head underwater, Kim thought, "Ice cream is going to be the death of me." Finally, with a huge effort, he managed to roll the kayak on his fourth try. He paddled, shivering and panting, to a nearby sandbar.

Half an hour later, the rest of the expedition floated around the bend. As one of its members recently recalled, "There sat Kim in the 120-degree sun, as calm as Buddha, cranking the handle of a gigantic ice cream maker."

"Were you angry that he'd taken off without the rest of you?" I asked.

"Not after the first spoonful."

NIGHT OWL

y husband and I sleep in a white wooden bed whose headposts are surmounted by two birds, carved and painted by an artist friend. On George's side there is a meadowlark, brown of back, yellow of breast, with a black pectoral V as trig and sporty as the neck of a tennis sweater. On my side there is a snowy owl, more muted in coloration, its feathers a frowzy tessellation of white and black. *Sturnella magna* and *Nyctea scandiaca* have one thing in common: they are both fast asleep, their eyes shut tight, their beaks resting peacefully on their breasts.

Alas, the lark and the owl who rest beneath their wooden familiars have a far harder time synchronizing their circadian rhythms. George is an early riser, a firm believer in seizing the day while it is still fresh. I am not fully alive until the sun sets. In the morning, George is quick and energetic, while I blink in the sunlight, move as if through honey, and pour salt in the coffee. When we turn off the light at 11:30—too late for him, too early for me—George falls instantly asleep, while I, mocked by the bird that slumbers above my head, arrange and rearrange the pillows, searching for the elusive cool sides.

In the fourth century B.C., Androsthenes, a scribe who accompanied Alexander the Great to India, observed that the tamarind tree opened its leaves during the day and folded them at night. He assumed that it was worshiping the sun. Twenty-two centuries later, the great Swedish taxonomist Carolus Linnaeus designed a flower clock—a circular garden whose twelve wedge-shaped flower beds, each planted with species whose petals opened at a different hour, told the time from 6:00 A.M. (white water lily) to 6:00 P.M. (evening primrose). In humans, the circadian clock is centered in the suprachiasmatic nucleus, a freckle-sized, sickle-shaped cluster of nerve cells in the hypothalamus, but it can be activated by proteins produced by genes all over the body. Scientists at Cornell have successfully reset human biological clocks (though only temporarily) by shining bright lights on the backs of people's knees, suggesting that the mechanisms for controlling sleeping and waking are embedded in nearly every human cell—as well as in every flower petal, every insect antenna, every bird wing.

Chronobiologists have also established that out of every ten people, eight follow a normal circadian cycle (that is, rising naturally at around 7:30 A.M.); one is a lark; and one is an owl. These settings are genetically encoded and cannot be erased. Once an owl, always an owl. (The same goes for other species. Wilse Webb, a psychologist at the University of Florida, spent five years trying to teach rats not to sleep between noon and 6:00 P.M. "They, by their contrary nature," he told Lynne Lamberg, an expert on sleep patterns, "spent five years teaching me otherwise.") I would wager my softest down pillow that the Cornell scientist who thought up the light-on-the-backs-of-the-knees experiment was an owl. At 8:00 A.M., could any biologist dream up something so lunatic (from *luna*, moon), so surreal, so redolent of the punchy wee hours and so incompatible with the rational light of morning?

"When I write after dark," observed Cyril Connolly, "the shades of evening scatter their purple through my prose. Then why not write in the morning? Unfortunately in my case there is never very much of the morning, and it is curious that although I do not despise people who go to bed earlier than I, almost everyone is impatient with me for not getting up." Connolly put his finger on the human owl's perennial problem. The natural world discovered the benefits of shift work long ago: it is easier to share a given territory when not everyone is out and about at once. No one faults the bandicoot for prowling after dusk; no one chides the night-flying cecropia moth for its decadence; no one calls the whippoorwill a lazy slugabed for sleeping by day and singing by night—but people who were born to follow similar rhythms are viewed by the other nine tenths of the population as a tad threadbare in the moral fiber department.

"Those who would bring great things to pass," cautioned the eighteenth-century theologian Matthew

Henry, "must rise early." In the medieval Benedictine horarium, the first of the monk's seven daily offices was observed at 3:15 A.M., the better to get a corner on virtue before anyone else could put in a competing bid. And at 4:30 A.M., is it any surprise that in 1660 one would have found John Milton, lustrous with matutinal rectitude, listening to a servant read aloud from the Hebrew Bible, while in 1890 one would have found the Irish journalist and pornographer Frank Harris (on the rare nights when he was sleeping alone) finally nodding off after a night of unspeakable debauch?

The owl's reputation may be beyond salvation. Who gets up early? Farmers, bakers, doctors. Who stays up late? Muggers, streetwalkers, cat burglars. It's assumed that if you're sneaking around after midnight, you must have something to hide. Night is the time of goblins, ghouls, vampires, zombies, witches, warlocks, demons, wraiths, fiends, banshees, poltergeists, werefolk, bogeymen, and things that go bump. (It is also the time of fairies and angels, but, like many comforting things, these are all too easily crowded out of the imagination. The nightmare trumps the pleasant dream.) Night, like winter, is a metaphor for death: one does not say "the dead of morning" or "the dead of spring." In a strange and tenebrous book called *Night* (which every lark should be forced to read, preferably by moonlight), the British critic A. Alvarez (an owl) points out, glumly, that Christ is known as the Light of the World and Satan as the Prince of Darkness. With such a powerful pro-lark tradition arrayed against us, must we owls be forever condemned to the infernal regions—which, despite their in-extinguishable flames, are always described as *dark*?

I have tried hard to understand the lark's perspective. Campbell Geeslin, the artist who carved our bedpost finials, retires at nine and rises at five. "I've gotten up early ever since I was a boy in West Texas," he told me. "You'd look out of the window at dawn, and the sky would stretch on forever. It was a special creamy color at that hour, before the clouds came. It was the only time when it was cool. The morning was clean and blank and full of promise, like a piece of paper no one had written on yet. I couldn't wait to jump out of bed and invent something: a car, an airplane, a vacuum cleaner made from a spice can. By sunset, the day was used up, exhausted. Night was a time of disappointment, when you thought about all the things you'd hoped to do and hadn't done. There's nothing as sad and lonely as the bark of a coyote somewhere off in the West Texas night, and the moon hanging outside your window as bone-white as an old cow skull."

That's persuasive testimony, but it's not going to make me jump out of bed at five any more than a panegyric by a white water lily on the splendors of the morning is going to make the evening primrose transplant itself in Linnaeus's 6:00 A.M. flower bed. My suprachiasmatic nucleus is stuck in the owl position, and there's nothing I can do about it. Dawns are all very well (though I generally see them after staying up all night, when I may be too sleepy to appreciate them), but they can't hold a candle to a full moon, an aurora borealis, a meteor shower, or a comet.

In March of 1986, I was climbing with a friend on the Tasman Glacier in New Zealand. It occurred to us that if we got up at 1:00 A.M. and walked northeast across the glacier, we might be able to see Halley's Comet, which was making its every-seventy-sixth-year swing that month and could be best viewed (or so we had read) from the Southern Hemisphere. For my larkish companion, 1:00 A.M. was an early start; for me, it was simply an excuse to postpone my bedtime. We left the Tasman Saddle promptly at one, roped up, and put on our crampons in what seemed at first like pitch darkness but soon, once our eyes grew accustomed to the light of thousands of stars reflected on the shimmering glacier, seemed more like dusk. After crunching a mile or so across the clean hard snow, which had been unpleasantly slushy in the afternoon sun, we stopped on a narrow col with a thousand-foot drop-off on either side. And there it was: a small white cornucopia above the northern horizon, not solid, but delicately stippled, as if produced by a heavenly dot-matrix printer. We spread our sleeping bags on the snow and crawled inside. The vantage point was dizzying. It was impossible to tell whether the comet was above us or we were above the comet; we were all falling through space, missing the stars by inches.

Surely the best thing about camping is the night. Night is what differentiates a camping trip from a series of day hikes. There are few greater pleasures than stretching out in your tent, inside which a glowing candle lantern makes your muddy boots and damp wool socks look as if they were painted by Georges de La Tour, and glimpsing, through the open flap, the corner of a constellation that is invisible from your hometown. (Since I live in New York City, that includes just about everything, even the Big Dipper.) There are sounds you wouldn't hear at home, either: crickets, cicadas, tree frogs, loons, owls—even, on a memorable Catskills backpacking trip in my husband's youth, the urgent rustles of copulating porcupines. The contrast between the infinite space outside the tent and the cozily delimited interior, whose little zippers and pouches (for glasses, handkerchiefs, pocketknives) form a miniature simulacrum of a well-ordered pantry, nudges my memory back to the houses I used to make in my childhood by suspending a blanket over a table, dragging in a tray of cocoa and cookies, and creating a private domestic zone in which the temperature was always warm and the light was always crepuscular. Hell may be a dark place, but so is the womb.

My husband inherited his larkishness, along with his Roman nose and his shaggy eyebrows, from his father, who would feel he had committed an act of irreparable sloth if he slept past 4:30 A.M. I inherited my owlishness from a father who shares Jimmy Walker's conviction that it is a sin to go to bed on the same day you get up. Even if he retires at 2:00 A.M., my father cannot fall asleep without at least an hour of rigorous mental games. (He is the sort of person who could never get drowsy counting sheep; he once told me that he just got wider and wider awake as the numbers mounted, since he had to make sure he was counting correctly.) He composes puns, limericks, clerihews, palindromes, anagrams, and alphabetical lists of various kinds. An example of the last of these genres: Excluding the refractory *x*, which was long ago thrown out of the game, proceed through the alphabet from *a* to *z*, finding words that end with the letters *el*. Proper names are allowed. Solution: Abel, babel, channel, diesel, Edel, Fidel, Gödel . . . and so on. The sailing was reasonably clear until my father got to *z*, a perennial troublemaker. It took an hour, from 4:00 A.M. to 5:00 A.M., to come up with the name of a fellow reviewer at *The Nation* whom he had last seen sixty years earlier: Morton Dauwen Zabel. My father says that at the moment Mr. Zabel sidled into his consciousness, he was suffused with a sense of transcendent completion greater than he had ever felt on signing a book contract or closing a deal.

Insomnia need not be disagreeable. When Annie Proulx can't sleep, she puts on Quebec reels and dances around for half an hour in her bunny slippers. Until the fantasy wore thin with repetition, F. Scott Fitzgerald quarterbacked the Princeton team to hundreds of nocturnal victories over Yale. Lewis Carroll, like my father, posed himself problems:

Q: If 70 per cent [of a group of pensioners] have lost an eye, 75 per cent an ear, 80 per cent an arm, 85 per cent a leg; what percentage, *at least*, must have lost all four?

A: Ten. Adding the wounds together, we get 70 + 75 +
  80 + 85 = 310, among 100 men; which gives 3 to each,
  and 4 to 10 men. Therefore the least percentage is 10.

Not everyone's cup of somnifacient tea—but, as Carroll
put it, "I believe that an hour of calculation is much better for me than half-an-hour of worry."

I feel certain that Morton Dauwen Zabel would never
have paid my father an extrasensory visit during the day,
nor would Lewis Carroll have performed his amputations
with such accuracy had he been operating when the rest
of the world was awake. Owls think better at night. It is
true, however, that many people make mistakes when
they stay up late. The *Exxon Valdez* ran aground at 12:04
A.M.; the pesticide tank at Bhopal ruptured at 12:40 A.M.;
the Chernobyl reactor exploded at 1:23 A.M.; the reactor
at Three Mile Island spewed radiation at 3:53 A.M. These
accidents were all attributable to human error. But surely
the errant humans were among the non-owl 90 percent:
day folk, maybe even dyed-in-the-wool larks, who had
been forced by the exigencies of shift work to disobey the
ticking of their circadian clocks. At Three Mile Island,
the workers had just rotated to the night shift *that very
day* and must have been as groggy as a planeful of New
Yorkers disembarking in Kuala Lumpur.

It was therefore with a distinct sense of unease that I
read *Night as Frontier*, a book by a Boston University sociologist named Murray Melbin. Melbin believes that
night, like the American West in the nineteenth century,
is a territory to be colonized. We have run out of space, so

if we wish to increase our productivity and uncrowd our cities, the only dimension we have left to occupy is time: the hours after the normal workday. Many factories have already discovered that it is cheaper to operate around the clock, even if wages are higher on the nonstandard shifts. If Melbin is right, those factory nightworkers— along with locksmiths, bartenders, bail bondsmen, twenty-four-hour gas-station attendants, police officers, paramedics, security guards, taxi drivers, talk-show hosts, and suicide hotline volunteers—are the advance wave of a vast nocturnal migration. There are many parallels between night work and the settlement of the Western frontier: the pioneers tend to be young and nonconformist (the middle-aged are home watching Jay Leno); the population is sparse (owls tend to be mavericks); authority is decentralized (supervisors are asleep); life is informal (no coats and ties are required); there is hardship (fatigue, isolation, disruption of family routines) and lawlessness (parking-lot muggings).

Melbin may be right. But in my view, if the night is like the Wild West, *let's leave it that way*. If too many settlers start putting down stakes in the territory beyond midnight, California is going to happen. The wide open spaces will become the Los Angeles freeway system, and with too few owls behind the wheel, there will be accidents.

Because I savor the illusion of having the small hours to myself, when I am in the city I prefer to spend them at home. The noirish melancholy of the after-hours club and the all-night diner suits many owls, but I'd rather be in our bedroom, looking out the window every once in a while at the flocks of chic, black-garbed young couples, their laughter floating upward through the night, who cross the patch of lamplight at Houston and West Broadway. Even if the city were safer, I doubt I would go for late walks. Dickens once had a period of insomnia during which he spent several nights walking the London streets between half past twelve and half past five: Haymarket, Newgate Prison, Bethlehem Hospital, Westminster Bridge, Covent Garden. He was searching for comfort but found only drunkards, thieves, rain, shadows, silence, and scudding clouds "as restless as an evil conscience in a tumbled bed." The night he described in *The Uncommercial Traveller* is not the sable goddess of Edward Young or the bare-bosomed nurturer that Walt Whitman beseeched to press him close; it is more like the horrid place of "distempered gloom of thought / And deadly weariness of heart" that James Thomson visited in "The City of Dreadful Night," the most depressing of all nocturnal poems. For Dickens, as for me, the urban night was best enjoyed indoors, preferably with a book in hand.

"There is absolutely no such thing as reading but by a candle," wrote Charles Lamb.

> We have tried the affectation of a book at noon-day in gardens, and in sultry arbours; but it was labour thrown away. Those gay motes in the beam come about you, hovering and teasing, like so many coquets, that will have you all to their self, and are jealous of your abstractions. By the midnight

taper, the writer digests his meditations. By the same light we must approach to their perusal, if we would catch the flame, the odour.

I prefer a 150-watt halogen bulb, but I know just what he meant. Reading by day seems prosaic and businesslike, the stuff of duty rather than of pleasure. When I was ten or twelve, I would close my schoolbooks without protest at bedtime, but after my mother left the room, I'd flip the switch of my bedside lamp and snatch a stolen hour (or two or three) of novel-reading, my heart beating wildly if I heard footsteps in the hall. Had my mother glimpsed the light under the door? She always had the grace to pretend she hadn't. Her steps would grow fainter, the book would grow shorter, and I would fall asleep at an ungodly hour, suffused with the goody-goody's secret pride at having sinned.

The child who reads at night is likely to become the adult who writes at night. During the day, I pop out of my chair a dozen times an hour. The phone rings, the fax beeps, the mailbox needs to be checked, the coffee needs to be brewed, the letter needs to be filed, the Post-its need to be rearranged—and possibly color-coded—*right this instant.* How can the writer's distractive sirens be resisted? During a phase when his muse was particularly obdurate, John McPhee used to tie himself to his chair with his bathrobe sash. Schiller heightened his powers of concentration by inhaling the fumes from a cache of rotten apples he kept in a drawer. All I need to do is stay up past midnight.

Something amazing happens when the rest of the world is sleeping. I am glued to my chair. I forget that I ever wanted to do anything but write. The crowded city, the crowded apartment, and the crowded calendar suddenly seem spacious. Three or four hours pass in a moment; I have no idea what time it is, because I never check the clock. If I chose to listen, I could hear the swish of taxis bound for downtown bars or the soft saxophone riffs that drift from a neighbor's window, but nothing gets through. I am suspended in a sensory deprivation tank, and the very lack of sensation is delicious.

A few years ago, I was inching along with excruciating slowness on a book I was trying to write. It was clear that the only way I would finish it was by surrendering unconditionally to my owl self. For several months, I worked all night, ate breakfast with my family, and slept from 9:00 A.M. to 4:00 P.M. The pages piled up as speedily as the Tailor of Gloucester's piecework. The only problem was that even though my husband and I inhabited the same zip code, he was living on New York time and I had apparently moved to Auckland. The jet lag on weekends was terrible.

I finished the book and promised I'd never do it again, except for occasional binges of three or four nights: just long enough to write an essay. I have kept my word. I am even more attached to George than I am to my circadian rhythm, so the trade-off has been worth it. And unlike most recovering alcoholics, I seem to be able to indulge in a bender now and then without permanently falling off the wagon.

It is now 3:42 A.M. Everyone here has been asleep for hours except my daughter's hamster, the other nocturnal mammal in the family, who is busy carrying sunflower seeds from one end of his terrarium to the other. After Silkie completes this task, he will change his mind and bring the seeds back again. I will do more or less the same thing with several paragraphs. Then, when the light breaks over Houston Street and the pigeons begin to coo on the window ledge, Silkie and I will retire. "And so by faster and faster degrees," wrote Dickens at the end of his long night walk, "until the last degrees were very fast, the day came, and I was tired and could sleep." Good night.

Procrustes and the
Culture Wars

O f all the serial killers who plied their trade in ancient Attica, Procrustes exercised the highest degree of professional ingenuity. "This man," wrote Diodorus Siculus, "used to take passing travelers and throw them upon a certain bed. When they were too big for it, he lopped off the overhanging parts of their bodies. When they were too small, he stretched them out by the feet." In Apollodorus's version, Procrustes had two beds, one large (on which he laid the short men, and hammered them until they were tall) and one small (on which he laid the tall men, and sawed them until they were short). Hyginus also belonged to the two-bed school, although he had Procrustes stretch his shorter victims by suspending anvils from their limbs. Whatever the furniture arrangement, everyone agreed that Procrustes' house was conveniently located on the road to Athens, and that when he offered his hospitality to footsore wayfarers, he was rarely refused.

Most later writers, including Plutarch, aligned themselves with Diodorus, perhaps believing (as do I) that a single bed for all comers was better suited to Procrustes' one-size-fits-all philosophy. I like to think, in fact, that the host was the *only* man who was exactly the right size for his bed, and that his unorthodox etiquette was a way of enforcing a solipsistic conformity: It fits me, therefore everyone should fit it.

The Procrustean bed, Diodorus model, suggests itself with dispiriting aptness as a metaphor for the Culture Wars, right down to the blandishments with which Procrustes must have lured his guests over the threshold. (I picture him as a handsome fellow with a large vocabulary and an oleaginous tongue, not unlike the chairmen of many English departments.) There's just one crucial difference. Sometimes Procrustes lopped off his victims, and sometimes he stretched them, but the Culture Wars always lop. I have never seen cultural politics enlarge a work of literature, only diminish it.

By the Culture Wars, I mean that peculiar development of the last two decades or so that takes culture—a multidimensional thing if there ever was one—and attempts to compress it to a skinny little line running from left to right. No matter how oddly shaped a book or a play or a poem is—no matter how idiosyncratic, how ambivalent, how anarchic, how complicated, how big, how messy—it's just got to fit that Procrustean bed. So out comes the handsaw, and WHOP! With a few quick strokes, it's cut down to size and, as a kind of casual side effect, murdered.

Both armies in the Culture Wars are eager to recruit

new soldiers for this limb-attenuation campaign. Here's how you enlist. Without giving it much thought, you toe the party line—once. You think you've signed your name to a single page, but then you discover that a thousand pages of carbon paper lie underneath, transferring your signature with perfect fidelity to a thousand different documents. With your collusion, cultural politics have become, in the words of the eighteenth-century poet David Mallet, a

> *Tyrant! more cruel than Procrustes old;*
> *Who, to his iron-bed, by torture fits,*
> *Their nobler part, the souls of suffering wits.*

You have lost your right to judge literary works on a case-by-case basis, and those works have lost whatever nuances were lodged in their overhanging periphery.

Reader, cast down your handsaw! You need not become a conscientious objector—there are plenty of ideas worth shedding blood for—but if in every battle you look around and see the same people fighting alongside you, you should ask yourself whether you are demonstrating an admirable constancy or a Procrustean intransigence. I do not suggest that the attractions of a single set of marching orders are easy to resist. It is far more work to start from scratch every time you open a book than to let someone else make up your mind before you read the first word. But if you start hacking the toes off your culture, you will soon look down and find that your own toes—those humble appendages, given to blisters and

bunions and ingrown nails, yet so essential to your bal-
ance—are unaccountably missing.

There are dozens of questions currently provoking
skirmishes in the Culture Wars. I propose to discuss four
elementary ones, all concerning the literary canon. I do
not expect everyone to agree with me, but I do hope to
show that it is possible for a single person to entertain
some ostensibly liberal views and some ostensibly conservative views and some utterly ambivalent views, and that
such inconsistency can have a wonderfully dulling effect
on the blade of Procrustes' handsaw.

S*hould we read great books because of their literary
value or because they provide moral lessons—that is, because they teach us how to live?*

When David Denby returned to Columbia at the age
of forty-eight to audit two Western civilization courses he
had originally taken three decades earlier, his literature
professor told the students on the first day of class,
"You're here for very selfish reasons. You're here to build
a self." That's a pretty clear summary of the moral-lesson
school.

Here's Hannah Arendt: "The trouble with the edu-
cated philistine was not that he read the classics, but that
he did so prompted by the ulterior motive of self-
perfection, remaining quite unaware of the fact that
Shakespeare or Plato might have to tell him more important things than how to educate himself." That's a pretty
clear summary of the literary school.

My view is that being forced to choose between the

two is a senseless act of sadomasochism that injures both reader and book. College students—over whose souls most of the goriest battles in the Culture Wars are fought—are, by virtue of their youth, deeply engrossed in character building. Is it wrong to enlist the help of Shakespeare and Plato in this difficult task? But if that's all that young readers do, then narcissism (*Should I emulate Tybalt or Mercutio? If I liberate my soul from dependence on my body, as the* Phaedo *suggests, can I still have sex with Tiffany?*) trumps aesthetics, and great books are reduced, by a process that trims away all the most beautiful parts, to self-help manuals.

These days, it is mostly the people who consider themselves to be on the cultural left who ally themselves with the self-builders, and mostly those on the right who accuse the self-builders of shallow egotism. This just shows how fickle the whole right-to-left spectrum is, for the self-building position used to be considered conservative. It was Matthew Arnold, that well-known revolutionary firebrand, who wrote "that poetry is at bottom a criticism of life; that the greatness of a poet lies in his powerful and beautiful application of ideas to life,—to the question: How to live." Whatever critical cycle we happen to have been born into, reading with only one motive in mind seems unnecessarily restrictive. However, to those who insist on a single path, I would recommend self-building. They will miss a great deal, but they will miss even more if their reading is a disembodied intellectual experience that has been carefully divorced from their own lives.

People who have concentrated on self-building

haven't turned out so badly. Consider the example of Vice Admiral James Stockdale, Ross Perot's running mate, whose favorite book was the *Enchiridion* of Epictetus. Judging from Stockdale's incoherence in the 1992 vice-presidential debate, I think it's fair to say that he didn't learn much about literary style from Epictetus. However, he did learn something about Arnold's "powerful and beautiful application of ideas to life."

Stockdale first read the *Enchiridion* at the age of thirty-eight, when the navy sent him to Stanford to study international relations, and Philip Rhinelander, the dean of humanities and sciences, invited him to take his philosophy course. Stockdale did so, received supplementary tutoring from Rhinelander, and found himself drawn to the Stoics. Rhinelander mentioned that Frederick the Great had always brought a copy of the *Enchiridion* on his military campaigns, so when Stockdale was sent to Vietnam, he took along the copy his professor had given him during their last meeting. In September of 1966, Stockdale's plane was hit by antiaircraft fire over North Vietnam, and as he was descending by parachute, knowing he was about to become a prisoner of war, he said to himself, "I'm leaving the world of technology and entering the world of Epictetus." I would venture a guess that this is the first time a parachutist has thought about first-century Stoic philosophy on the way down. Stockdale didn't have his copy of the *Enchiridion* with him, but he hardly needed to, since by that time he had the book virtually memorized.

Epictetus, born as a slave in Phrygia and sold to Nero's

secretary, is said to have once murmured quietly to his master, who was twisting his leg, "You will break it." When the leg broke, he said with a smile, "Did I not tell you that you would do so?" Stockdale contemplated this incident during seven years as a prisoner of war, four of which were spent in solitary confinement and two in leg irons. He also pondered the following passages, among others:

> Work, therefore, to be able to say to every harsh appearance, "You are but an appearance, and not absolutely the thing you appear to be." And then examine it by those rules which you have, and first, and chiefly, by this: whether it concerns the things which are in our own control, or those which are not; and, if it concerns anything not in our control, be prepared to say that it is nothing to you.

> Sickness is a hindrance to the body, but not to your ability to choose, unless that is your choice. Lameness is a hindrance to the leg, but not to your ability to choose.

> Let death and exile, and all other things which appear terrible be daily before your eyes, but chiefly death, and you will never entertain any abject thought, nor too eagerly covet anything.

> Upon all occasions we ought to have these [words of Socrates] ready at hand: . . . "O Crito, if it thus pleases the gods, thus let it be. Anytus and Melitus may kill me indeed, but hurt me they cannot."

It was in this way that, through more than fifteen episodes of torture, Stockdale was able to preserve the self that Epictetus had helped him build. When he was released by Hanoi in 1973, he was lame, just as Epictetus was when he was released from slavery in Rome, but, like his exemplar, he believed that his external suffering had failed to destroy his internal sense of freedom. I can think of worse ways to use literature.

Should the life of the writer affect our valuation of the work? In other words, if the writer was a stinker, do we boot the book out of the canon? Or, as *The New York Times Magazine* put it in an article about Herman Melville, "Forget the whale. The big question is: Did he beat his wife?"

No one will ever be certain, but according to family rumors, long suppressed by scholars who wished to protect his reputation, Melville chased his wife, Elizabeth, around the table with a carving knife and once, when drunk, pushed her down the back stairs. At the very least, he made her so miserable that, in 1867, her family made abortive plans to help her escape her marriage via a feigned kidnapping. Even Hershel Parker, Melville's most devoted biographer, admitted to Philip Weiss, the author of the *Times* article, "One of the great-grandchildren told me a story that Melville came home once with a bag of oranges and ate them by himself in front of his daughter." That's not the sort of crime that lands a man in jail, but Melville's daughter was *hungry*, and after you hear a few stories like that, it is no longer possible to think of Melville as someone you'd like to invite to supper.

But should we forget the whale? That is, if Melville did push Lizzie down the stairs, should the stock of *Moby-Dick* experience a parallel plummet? In similar fashion, we now know that Byron committed incest and pedophilia, T. S. Eliot and Ezra Pound were anti-Semites, and Philip Larkin was a more democratic sort of bigot (he hated almost everybody). Should their poetry be permanently tainted by their character deficiencies?

These questions seem to me to be intertwined with the question of whether we should read great books for their literary merit or for the purpose of self-building, and to provide a compelling argument for doing both. Those who believe that the purpose of literature is primarily moral are going to run into trouble if the book they've been using as a guide to living turns out to have been written by someone who beat his wife. I'm sure it mattered to James Stockdale that Epictetus was an exemplary man—that he is said to have lived by choice in a small hut furnished with only a pallet and a lamp, that he adopted a child who would otherwise have been left to die. It would have been acutely disturbing to find out, for example, that Epictetus had abused that child.

Unsurprisingly, it is the self-builders who tend to place a great deal of emphasis on biography and who vote to expel someone from the canon if he or she turns out to have been an unsavory character. But if you believe, as I do, that great literature can be written by bad people, then your library can remain intact, no matter how much respect you lose for the authors as individuals.

Some readers feel that the life is irrelevant and *only* the work counts. A friend schooled in the New Criticism recently wrote me: "As a critic I was trained to ignore the biography of the author. We figured he knew what he was doing; it was our job to figure it out. To slide into biographical details was to admit a lack of critical perception. Let the work stand for the man." I disagree. For instance, if you know that Melville was a terrible husband, you may be able to make more sense of the sealed-off, seabound world of *Moby-Dick*, where everybody was male, even the whale. And even if there are no themes in the work that resonate with the life, great writers are not machines that produce, out of nothingness, a series of words that happen to be more perfect than other people's words; they are flawed mortals, often imprudent and uncivil, who are so large (that's what greatness *is*: size) that every part of them deserves to be understood.

S*hould a book be demoted if its plot fails to meet standards of behavior that have changed since it was written?*

I once read a letter to *The New York Times Book Review* in which Sharon Uemura Ronholt of Stockton, California, berated Richard Jenkyns for his review of Robert Fagles's translation of the *Odyssey*. She wrote, "Nowhere in his review does Mr. Jenkyns draw critical attention to the fact that Homer's world is that of a quintessential male fantasy and may not meet with universal approbation: Homer's hero commits adultery with various gorgeous, high-class women, and the construction of the plot (his desire to depart for 'home') legitimizes his callous abandonment of his ever-changing women lovers." Ms.

Ronholt therefore concluded that it was naïve and, as she termed it, "pretheoretical" to accept the *Odyssey* as "a 'timeless' Great Book."

Sharon Uemura Ronholt put her finger on the paradox that women, or indeed anyone who is currently better off than he or she would have been in another century or another place, will always feel when reading works from other times or cultures. But she didn't see it as a paradox, a word that suggests ambivalence. She saw it as an unambiguous black mark against the *Odyssey*.

Whenever I read Homer, I see ample evidence that women were treated abominably in ancient Greece, and I am very thankful that I live now and not then. In fact, I would rather pay a visit to Procrustes than marry any of Homer's heroes. Fortunately, none of them is asking me. The invitation Homer offers me is a far broader one: to enter a world that was very different from ours, but that in its own "pretheoretical" way possessed nobility and beauty. If I had to step into a polling booth and vote on Homer's sexual politics, I'd pull the NO lever strenuously. I am therefore very glad that the *Odyssey* is a poem, not a referendum.

I would guess that Ms. Ronholt doesn't much like *The Adventures of Huckleberry Finn*, either. If you're on the cultural right these days, you're supposed to think it's a masterpiece—the book from which, as Ernest Hemingway said, all modern American literature has come. (Of course, if you were on the cultural right a century ago, you would probably have disliked the book and considered its author—a muckraker who had uncovered political corruption in San Francisco and would later denounce King Leopold's regime in the Congo—an untrustworthy radical. A month after publication, *Huckleberry Finn* was banished from the public library in Concord, Massachusetts, on the ground that it was "trash and suitable only for the slums.")

If you're on the cultural left today, you're supposed to think that *Huckleberry Finn* should be expunged from the reading lists of America's high schools, partly because it contains the word *nigger* and partly because nineteenth-century progressives don't sound like late-twentieth-century progressives. In a controversial 1996 article in *Harper's* called "Say It Ain't So, Huck," Jane Smiley wrote that she was "stunned" by the idea "that this is a great novel, that this is even a serious novel." According to Smiley, one of the book's disqualifying flaws is Huck's decision to take Jim down the Mississippi River instead of across it to Illinois. She sees this as a moral failure on Huck's part, and therefore on Mark Twain's part as well.

"So Jane Smiley would have crossed the Mississippi to the free state of Illinois with her Jim and freed him without delay," responded a reader named Anson J. Cameron. (Mr. Cameron hails from Port Melbourne, Australia, and may thus be above the American fray.)

And if she kept her description of the river and the Southern sky to a minimum and the dialogue to just a few mutterings from her Huck about how many slaveholders' houses he was set to raze, she could probably free Jim inside of a page. Now, supposing she could keep writing (and

Huck could keep rowing) at this pace, she might invent and free upwards of three hundred slaves in the course of her Huck Finn, whereas Twain, farting around with humor and other such distractions, only got around to freeing one.

I'm with Mr. Cameron. I'm very grateful that Huck Finn and Mark Twain were so inefficient and unethical that they didn't manage to wind up their book on page 54, a few paragraphs after the raft sets off down the river. (And that Homer didn't send Odysseus straight home.)

What *should you do when a work's language excludes you?* If the very words leave you on the sidelines—because, for instance, they are addressed to men and you are a woman—should you stick out your tongue and say, "Well, if that's the way you feel about it, I reject you, too"?

Consider, for example, "The American Scholar," the Harvard Phi Beta Kappa oration that Ralph Waldo Emerson delivered on August 31, 1837, in the Brattle Street Church in Cambridge, Massachusetts. He spoke for an hour and a quarter on the necessity of emancipating America's intellectual tradition from "the sere remains of foreign harvests." The audience included Oliver Wendell Holmes, James Russell Lowell, Richard Henry Dana, Edward Everett Hale, and plenty of famous people who had only two names. Not everyone was impressed. Hale wrote in his diary that Emerson was "half-crazy" and that his speech was "not very good and very transcendental." But

Lowell called the event "a scene to be always treasured in the memory for its picturesqueness and its inspiration," and Holmes later referred to the oration as "our Intellectual Declaration of Independence." When Thomas Carlyle was sent a copy, he wrote to Emerson, "I could have *wept* to read that speech; the clear high melody of it went tingling thro' my heart; I said to my wife 'There, woman!' She read; and returned and charges me to return for answer, 'that there had been nothing met with like it since Schiller went silent.' My brave Emerson!"

The day I learned I was to edit *The American Scholar*, a journal that takes its name from that very speech, I ran to my bookcase, pulled out a volume of my brave Emerson, and opened it to his Phi Beta Kappa oration. I expected, like Carlyle, to hear a clear high melody tingling thro' my heart. Instead, I read the following sentence: "In the right state [the scholar] is *Man Thinking*." This is the most famous line in the essay; it was used as *The American Scholar*'s epigraph until 1976. The first time I read it, I had skated over the phrase, assuming that "Man" was one of those capacious linguistic tents that had once had room for everybody, the way *horsemanship* included horsewomanship and *mankind* included womankind.

On this reading, however, I could see that Emerson really meant *Man* Thinking. Later in his speech he specifically distinguished the scholar from the "protected class" of "children and women"; they lived under a different tent. So what lesson was I to draw? Even though Emerson supported women's property rights and counted Margaret Fuller and Harriet Martineau among his friends and didn't complain when his wife served leg of lamb twenty days in a row, was I nonetheless compelled to write him off as a wicked misogynist and cast him from my bookshelf? No.

But if I left him on my shelf, did that mean I was forever excluded from the Emersonian fellowship, forced to press my nose against the glass of American intellectual life, as if the Man Thinking Club were a beer-swilling fraternity that invited me on the premises only on Saturday night? No.

One of the convenient things about literature is that, despite copyrights—which in Emerson's case expired long ago—a book belongs to the reader as well as to the writer. The greater the work, the wider the ownership, which is why there are such things as criticism, revisionism, and Ph.D. dissertations. I will not ask the sage of Concord to rewrite his oration. He will forever retain the right to speak his own words and to mean what he wished to mean, not what I would wish him to mean. But I will retain the right to recast Man Thinking in *my* mind as Curious People Thinking, because time has passed, and the tent has grown larger.

As we wrangle with these canonic questions, it may be useful to remember that this is not the first Culture War. In seventeenth-century France, Boileau and La Fontaine exchanged a notorious series of barbs with Fontenelle and Perrault in the Querelle des Anciens et des Modernes, a dispute over which was superior, classical or modern literature. The "Ancients" argued that Greece and Rome provided the only worthy literary models; the "Moderns" argued that if Descartes had improved on ancient science, his literary contemporaries might improve on ancient poetry. The quarrel spread across the Channel to England, where Sir William Temple took up the ancient cause, William Wotton took up the modern cause, and Jonathan Swift satirized them both in *A Full and True Account of the BATTEL Fought last FRIDAY, Between the* Antient *and the* Modern *BOOKS in St. JAMES's LIBRARY.*

"The present quarrel," wrote Swift, "is so inflamed by the warm heads of either faction, and the pretensions *somewhere or other* so exorbitant, as not to admit the least overtures of accommodation. This quarrel first began (as I have heard it affirmed by an old dweller in the neighbourhood) about a small spot of ground, lying and being upon one of the two tops of the hill Parnassus." The higher Parnassian summit was occupied by the Ancients, the lower by the Moderns. The Moderns, deciding that the Ancient peak was blocking their view, suggested that their neighbors either decamp to a lower altitude or permit the Moderns to carry over a few shovels and "level the said hill as low as they shall think it convenient." The Ancients declined; the Moderns were indignant; and a war broke out in which

whole rivulets of ink have been exhausted, and the virulence of both parties enormously augmented. Now, it must here be understood that ink is the great missive weapon in

all battles of the learned, which, conveyed through a sort of
engine called a quill, infinite numbers of these are darted
at the enemy by the valiant on each side, with equal skill
and violence, as if it were an engagement of porcupines.

According to Swift, the Parnassian turf battle produced a series of quarrelsome books, "known to the
world under several names, as *disputes, arguments, rejoin-
ders, brief considerations, answers, replies, remarks, reflections, objections, confutations,*" which, when admitted
to libraries, soon found themselves continuing the fray,
this time over the more general question of merit. The
conflict was bloody but spectacularly incompetent. Aris-
totle aimed an arrow at Bacon but instead shot Descartes
in the eye; Cowley dropped his shield and was sliced in
half by Pindar. Swift never revealed which side won, for
could anything but a stalemate result from demanding
that the world's readers choose A or B, not A and B, or A,
B, C, and Z? That binary view of culture was just as re-
ductive in 1697 as it is now, when the battle between the
Ancients and Moderns is still raging (except that Aris-
totle and Bacon now find themselves fighting on the
same side and being commanded to take potshots at Virginia Woolf).

The rivulets of ink still flow, and the battlefields of
the Culture Wars are still strewn with corpses. "Anger
and fury," observed Swift, "though they add strength to
the sinews of the body, yet are found to relax those of the
mind." The anger is real, but I believe that our wars, like
Swift's, are a fiction: a theoretical—or, as Sharon Uemura

Ronholt would put it, a "posttheoretical"—construct that would appall many of the writers over whose words the armies of the left and the right are trading grapeshot.

In order to analyze their strategies, let us return, in a pretheoretical way, to Procrustes—or rather to his nemesis, Theseus. It was Theseus who slew Procrustes on his own bed, though it is not recorded whether he stretched his ill-mannered host or lopped him off. Procrustes was not the only unpleasant character Theseus encountered while he was walking from the Peloponnesus to Athens. There were five others, and it seems to me that, with a little Procrustean stretching, they might represent the various hazards you are likely to encounter as a literary wayfarer wending your way through the obstacle course of the Culture Wars.

The first rogue was Periphetes the Club-Bearer, who had the ungallant habit of beating travelers to death with a giant bronze club. Theseus, never known for his subtlety, grabbed the club himself and bashed Periphetes over the head with it. Theseus was apparently so pleased with Periphetes' club that he stole it and carried it around with him for the rest of his life. This episode reminds me of how the right berated the left for politicizing culture, and then appropriated the weapon of politicization in order to bash the left over the head with it. I don't recommend that you follow suit.

The second was named Sinis the Pine-Bender. Sinis liked to bend two trees down to the ground, tie his victim to them, and let go. The trees sprang back in opposite directions, and the victim was torn in half. Surely these two trees are the political poles, each pantingly eager to embrace you, with the danger that you, too, will end up in pieces.

Theseus dismembered Sinis with his own pine trees, and then, after persuading Sinis's daughter that he would treat her honorably, he seduced, impregnated, and abandoned her. It's no wonder that the next challenge Theseus encountered was an angry female: the Wild Sow of Crommyon, a monstrous pig that was rampaging around the countryside, terrorizing local farmers. Who could the Wild Sow be but every male academic's nightmare of the enraged feminist who is barging her way into the very tenure slot he covets? Theseus responded to the Wild Sow of Crommyon as we would all like to respond to what we most fear: he killed her.

After she was out of the way, he met a murderer named Sciron. Sciron required his visitors to wash his feet, and when the ablution was complete, he kicked them off a cliff into the Saronic Gulf, where they were eaten by a giant turtle. Sciron could be none other than the forces that want you to take books that have always been an intimate part of your life, such as *Huckleberry Finn*, and kick them out of the canon. The giant turtle would make the Huck critics particularly happy, because if Huck Finn were not only banished but actually digested, there would be no danger of his ever creeping back into the canon.

After Theseus got rid of Sciron, he met Cercyon the Wrestler, whom of course he outwrestled. I like to think of Cercyon as your own conscience, with which you will

often wrestle as you grapple with these slippery and vex-
ing questions of culture and morality. I hope, however,
that, unlike Theseus, you do not choke your conscience to
death.

Now let us imagine that, as a modern-day Theseus
negotiating the thorny path of cultural politics, you have
somehow managed to resist all these dangers, perhaps
with a shade more finesse than your predecessor. Athens
is still far away, and you are exhausted. What do you
think you would long for most in all the world?

A bed, of course.

And that is just what Procrustes offers you. A soft bed,
I am sure, with 600-thread-count Egyptian cotton sheets,
a high-loft duvet, and goose-down pillows.

Don't lie down.

COLERIDGE THE RUNAWAY

n 1779, when Samuel Taylor Coleridge was seven, he asked his mother to slice him some cheese for toasting: "no easy matter, it being a *crumbly* cheese." His older brother Frank, his great rival in the family, sneaked into the kitchen and minced the cheese into tiny, untoastable pieces. Sam flew at Frank; Frank pretended to be seriously hurt; when Sam bent over him with fearful solicitude, Frank laughed and punched him in the face. At this juncture, Sam grabbed a kitchen knife and was on the verge of reducing his brother to the same condition as the cheese when their mother, the decorous wife of a Devonshire vicar, walked in. "I expected a flogging," recalled the thwarted murderer fifteen years later, "& struggling from her I ran away, to a hill at the bottom of which the Otter flows."

Coleridge spent a stormy night on the riverbank, shivering with cold and fright but reflecting "*at the same time* with inward & gloomy satisfaction, how miserable my Mother must be!" Dozens of villagers combed the churchyard, scoured the streets, dragged the ponds and the millrace. The fugitive awoke at 5:00 A.M., too chilled to move. "I saw the Shepherds & Workmen at a distance—& cryed but so faintly, that it was impossible to hear me 30 yards off—and there I might have lain & died—for I was now almost given over." His cries were finally heard by the local squire, Sir Stafford Northcote, who had been searching all night. "He carried me in his arms, for near a quarter of a mile; where we met my father & Sir Stafford's Servants," wrote Coleridge. "I remember, & never shall forget, my father's face as he looked upon me while I lay in the servant's arms— so calm, and the tears stealing down his face: for I was the child of his old age.—My Mother, as you may suppose, was outrageous with joy. . . . I was put to bed—& recovered in a day or so—but I was certainly injured— For I was weakly, & subject to the ague for many years after."

It was the first time, but not the last, that Coleridge ran away. Each successive escape recapitulated pieces of the pattern established in this archetypical truancy: misbehavior; flight; an absence charged with both misery and pleasure; rescue; illness; a tenderly supervised convalescence. The upshot was that he wriggled out of any number of tight spots, but, as often happens when one evades an unpleasant consequence, he was usually overtaken by another, larger one.

Coleridge's night on the riverbank is retold near the beginning of Richard Holmes's two-volume biography, a

work so vital that it sucks the air out of the readers'
"real" world, rendering it torpid by comparison, and
draws us into a parallel world that seems infinitely richer
in oxygen. (This is, of course, exactly what Coleridge did
in "Kubla Khan" and "Christabel," whose dreamscapes
are vivid enough to trump reality.) That a book should be
more compelling than its readers' lives is in itself no
proof of great art. The young mother who ignores her
crying baby because she is engrossed in *As the World
Turns*, the teenage boy who neglects his homework because he is busy decapitating cybermonsters, the driver
who misses his exit because his favorite song comes on
the radio—all have experienced, in ruder forms, something akin to what I felt on reading *Coleridge*. The difference is not just that Holmes is a wonderful writer;
it is that he invites us to enter a real life and live it,
year by year, alongside a real person. It is impossible to
read this book without forming opinions of Coleridge's
friends as if they were one's own: Charles Lamb is a
brick, Robert Southey a bluenose, William Hazlitt an
ingrate, William Wordsworth an egotist. (The essential
Coleridge-and-Wordsworth scene: A soirée at the Lambs'.
Coleridge sits at one end of the dinner table, quoting
Wordsworth. Wordsworth sits at the other end, quoting
Wordsworth.) And it is impossible to read this book without imagining what it would be like to talk with Coleridge (dazzling), have him as a houseguest (arduous),
walk with him in the Lake Country (fun for the first
forty miles), lie with him in a field to study the moonlight (damp).

I half-woke one morning recently with an obscure sense of dread, nagged by the feeling that someone close to me was in trouble. I knew that soon I would be sufficiently alert to remember who it was and to start making plans to help him, plans that I feared would be difficult and complex and likely to swallow up my day. I turned over in bed and saw volume 2 of *Coleridge* on my bedside table. It was open to page 350. When I had left him at midnight, Coleridge was lying in a sweat-soaked bed at the Grey Hound Inn in Bath, in December 1813, having argued with two housemates and fled into the night. He was nearly penniless; had missed the last stagecoach and walked five miles in a rainstorm, dragging a bag of books and old clothes; had a terrible cold; and was hallucinating from an opium overdose.

I was relieved. The runaway was someone else's responsibility. Nonetheless, I was unable to settle down to work until I had read far enough ahead to assure myself that Coleridge would be properly taken care of. (As usual, he was. A benevolent local doctor looked after him for two weeks until a rich businessman of Coleridge's acquaintance removed the patient to his house in Bristol. There Coleridge remained for nine months, sharing his capacious bedroom with a manservant specifically charged with suicide prevention. He complained of gout, kidney stones, erysipelas, stricture of the urethra, cirrhosis of the liver, and "angry Itching," from at least some of which, along with opium withdrawal and hypochondriasis, he actually suffered. A year later, restored to health, he commenced writing the *Biographia Literaria*.)

Coleridge's greatest escape took place in 1793, when he was twenty-one. He was a student at Cambridge, deep in debt, racked with the pains of unrequited love, and frequently drunk. His mortifications ("Mine is a sensibility gangrened with inward corruption") came to a head with the customary decision to run away. William Godwin described what happened: "spends a night in a house of ill-fame, ruminating in a chair: next morning meditates suicide, walks in the park, enlists, sleeps 12 hours on the officer's bed, and upon awaking is offered his liberty, which from a scruple of honour he refuses—marched to Reading—dinnerless on Christmas day, his pocket having been picked by a comrade."

Coleridge had accepted a bounty of six and a half guineas to enlist as a private in the 15th Light Dragoons, under the alias Silas Tomkyn Comberbache. A time-honored way to run away from oneself is, of course, to change one's name. Coleridge never liked "Samuel": "such a vile short plumpness, such a dull abortive smartness in the first Syllable, & this so harshly contrasted by the obscurity & indefiniteness of the syllable Vowel, and the feebleness of the uncovered liquid, with which it ends." In his private notebooks, he referred to himself as S.T.C. or Essteesee; as a writer, he used the pseudonyms Aphilos, Cordomi, Cuddy, Gnome, Idolo-clastes Satyrane, Laberius, Nehemiah Higginbottom, Nicias Erythraeus, Ventifrons, and Zagri. Private Comberbache was his most hapless alter ego, a man spectacularly unsuited to his post, barely able to ride a horse and subject to saddle sores that "grimly constellated my Posteriors," but beloved by his fellow soldiers. In a 1931 essay, E. M. Forster described the young recruit thus:

> He talked and laughed, didn't mind being teased, changed from subject to subject; he was superb; nothing could stop him when once he had started, and if asked to write a letter for you it was the same: the ink poured out in a torrent, so that by the time she had got to the fourth page the girl couldn't do otherwise than give in. . . . [His] idea that a horse ought to "rub himself down and so shine in all his native beauty"—well, it was the idea of a zany, still when the letter was written and the girl on the way there or back there was no reason you shouldn't brighten his horse up for him; it didn't take long, and you knew which end kicked and which bit, more than he did.

Private Comberbache was eventually removed from his horse and assigned to care for a trooper with smallpox. For eight days and eight nights he and his "poor Comrade" were quarantined in the Pest House, a tiny hut at whose door food and water were left by soldiers too frightened to enter. Comberbache was the perfect nurse, comforting the patient during fevers and hallucinations, "the putrid smell and the fatiguing Struggles."

The experience of nursing and being nursed was to become a recurrent theme in Coleridge's life and work. In the sickroom, he performed equally well horizontally and vertically. As a patient, he surrendered blissfully to what Charles Lamb called the "magnificent dream" of illness, whether he was being nursed as a

child after his night on the riverbank or lying with his
gouty leg propped up on Wordsworth's sofa while the
women of the house stroked and tickled him. But whenever the tables were turned, he exhibited both sympathy
and fortitude. When his brother-in-law Robert Lovell
was dying of fever, he sat with him all night; when his
young protégé Charles Lloyd had epileptic seizures, he
gently restrained him; toward the end of his life, when
his son Derwent had typhus, he hovered over his bed day
and night, sponging his face and forcing him to drink water. On the twenty-third day of Derwent's fever, he
recorded in his notebook, by candlelight, that he had
"Turned a poor (very large & beautiful) Moth out of the
Window in a hard Shower of Rain to save it from the
Flames!"

Derwent and the moth survived. Twenty-eight years
earlier, so had the trooper with smallpox. Silas Tomkyn
Comberbache was himself eventually saved by his brothers, who raised the money to bail him out of his regiment. He returned to Cambridge (late, because he went
for a walk and missed the carriage), vowed to rise at six
and abjure drunken parties, worked hard for a time, and
dropped out.

None of us knows anyone even remotely like Samuel
Taylor Coleridge. But all of us know someone very much
like Silas Tomkyn Comberbache, the fellow who makes
scads of promises he can't keep, ducks his responsibilities,
never pays his bills, moves through life in a cyclone of
disorganization, and yet—because he is generous, because he has so much charm, because he is his own worst

critic, because we can't help ourselves—commands and deserves our love.

The Comberbache side was clearly in charge when, as a young student at Christ's Hospital, Coleridge was walking through the Strand, oblivious to his surroundings, pretending to be Leander crossing the Hellespont. While making energetic swimming motions, he touched a stranger's coat and was accused of being a pickpocket. (But when the tearful boy explained that he was en route from Abydos to Sestos, the gentleman was so amazed by his eloquence that, instead of reporting him to the police, he paid for his membership in a circulating library.) The boy grew into a man who overslept, missed his deadlines, was afraid to open letters lest they contain bad news, and, according to Holmes, during a period when he was living alone, "started with six shirts, lost three in the laundry, found he had been sleeping in the fourth, and had inadvertently used the fifth as a floormat while washing." (But, wearing the sixth shirt, he gave a series of brilliant *ex tempore* lectures, the secret of whose success was their very lack of preparation.) He made plans for innumerable projects that were never realized: the Pantisocracy, a kibbutz-like commune on the Susquehanna River; a chemistry laboratory; a 1,400-page work of geography; a two-volume history of English prose; a monograph on poetry; a critique of Chaucer; a translation of *Faust*; a musical play about Adam and Eve; a history of logic; a history of German metaphysics; a treatise on witchcraft;

an epic on the fall of Jerusalem; an encyclopedia. At the end of one poetic fragment, he jotted, "*Meant* to have been finished, but *somebody* came *in*, or something *fell* out—& tomorrow—alas! Tomorrow!" (But he wrote poems, plays, essays, reviews, letters, journals, lectures, sermons, pamphlets, translations, newspaper articles, position papers, and civil decrees: enough to make Virginia Woolf call him "not a man, but a swarm.")

In 1797, Coleridge walked fifty miles to pay his first visit to Wordsworth, beginning a thirty-seven-year friendship broken by lovers' quarrels as tragic and passionate as if they had been romantic and not merely Romantic. Wordsworth recalled that as Coleridge approached the house, he "did not keep to the high road, but leaped over a gate and bounded down a pathless field by which he cut off an angle." Some years later, Hazlitt noted that both men liked to compose poetry while walking, but Coleridge preferred "uneven ground, or breaking through the straggling branches of a copse-wood; whereas Wordsworth always wrote (if he could) walking up and down a straight gravel-walk." Wordsworth did what was expected, and it was always correct and on time. According to Southey, Coleridge "does nothing that he ought to do, and everything which he ought not," and that is why his path was always more difficult and usually more interesting.

Even though Wordsworth expelled "Christabel" from the *Lyrical Ballads*, their collaborative collection, and demoted "The Rime of the Ancient Mariner" from the front to the back of volume 1; even though he accused

Coleridge of "a derangement in his intellectual and moral constitution"; even though, speaking from years of exhausted experience as Coleridge's host, he warned a hospitable barrister not to take their mutual friend into his household, and thereby precipitated "a compressing and strangling Anguish" that brought Coleridge to the brink of suicide—still, no one can deny that each man bored irretrievably to the center of the other's heart. Coleridge had a habit of getting close to his male friends by falling in love with the women in their orbits. His first love, Mary Evans, was the sister of a Christ's Hospital chum. The woman he married, Sara Fricker, was the sister of women who married two fellow Pantisocrats. And the object of years of unconsummated extramarital fantasies ("my whole Being wrapt up in one Desire, all the Hopes & Fears, Joys & Sorrows, all the Powers, Vigour & Faculties of my Spirit abridged into one perpetual Inclination"), and of many fine poems, was Sara Hutchinson, the sister of the woman who married William Wordsworth. One cannot help thinking that much of Coleridge's emotional attachment to Wordsworth was channeled into his yearning for the woman he anagrammed into "Asra," in order to distinguish her from the Sara he wished he had never married.

Poor Sara Fricker Coleridge! Coleridge had expected to live with her in America, demonstrating the perfectibility of Man in the great communal Pantisocracy. Instead, they shared an isolated cottage near Bristol and rapidly discovered that they had nothing in common. Sara was an honorable woman, a good mother, far from stupid, and beautiful in her youth; but she cared little for literature and was repelled by Coleridge's wild vagaries of mood. In 1798, after three years of marriage, Coleridge escaped her by traveling with Wordsworth to Germany, where he planned to stay three months and stayed ten. In 1804, he set off for six or eight months in Malta and Italy and stayed for two and a half years. After his return, Wordsworth observed that "he dare not go home, he recoils so much from the thought of domesticating with Mrs Coleridge." For the rest of his life, Coleridge lived apart from his wife and rarely saw his children. In one of the most sweeping rants ever uttered by a disappointed husband, he blamed his marriage's "endless *heart-wasting*" for his "irresolution, procrastination, [and] languor," as well as for his opium addiction and the loss of his poetic muse.

"No one on earth has ever LOVED me," he later wrote. I am sure that thousands of his readers, especially young women, have come upon that sentence and mentally piped up, "I have!" No attractive runaway—the more vulnerable, the better—will ever be in want of rescuers of a certain type. When I was in college, I was among the multitudes who wanted to sit at Coleridge's feet while he recited "The Eolian Harp," soothe his fevered brow, discuss metaphysics (even though I didn't know what they were), and create a domestic paradise from which he would never wish to flee. Didn't I think Asra might pose a bit of a threat? Not at all; Coleridge's daughter had called her "dumpy." I recently corresponded with the critic Evelyn Toynton about our favorite scapegrace, and was not surprised when she wrote, "I developed my crush on him in my first year of college and decided that if only he had been married to me instead of his unsympathetic wife, all his genius would have been realized." Back then, Evelyn kept a framed portrait of Coleridge at her bedside. It has since been retired, but her computer screen saver consists of three red words that scroll endlessly across a black background: "Silas Tomkyn Comberbache."

I asked Evelyn what she thought Coleridge was running away from, beyond the obvious—unhappy marriage, adult responsibilities, money problems, broken friendships, physical pain, unrealized ambitions, England's imaginative constraints. She responded:

> Could one say he was escaping from pain and self-loathing and the pain of self-loathing? Yet it seems to me that his escapism was extraordinary in that it was fueled (at least sometimes) by such a tremendous sense of what he was fleeing *toward*—feelings of transcendence, a state of oneness with the deity, a non-material reality far finer than the gross corporeality of the body, etc. etc. That's why there is always something reductive about those studies of S.T.C. that present him as, in effect, a typical junkie. Maybe, like every junkie, he just wanted to get high, but what got him high was of a higher order than with any other junkie one can think of.

The junkie label is from the opium, of course—and from "Kubla Khan," which, because it was composed under the influence, I once used as ammunition in an adolescent debate with my parents over the benefits of hallucinogenic drugs. It would be easy enough to romanticize their effects if you read only the first three or four hundred of Holmes's 1,031 pages. Coleridge savors the "beauteous spectra of two colours, orange and violet" in his tumbler of laudanum (opium dissolved in alcohol, available from any corner chemist). When he writes a friend, "Do bring down some of the Hyoscyamine Pills & I will give a fair Trial of opium, Hensbane, & Nepenthe," he sounds as cheery as Timothy Leary inviting Richard Alpert over for a few tabs of acid with a chaser of psilocybin. But in volume 2, opium becomes the stuff of the very nightmares he hoped it would suppress, "an indefinite indescribable Terror as with a scourge of ever restless, ever coiling and uncoiling Serpents." This is not the kind of escape I had in mind at sixteen. Nor did I have in mind the blocked bowels—a side effect of opium addiction—that made him "weep & sweat & moan & scream."

In 1816, when Coleridge was forty-three, his physician wrote a letter to James Gillman, a newly elected member of the Royal College of Surgeons, about an unnamed "unfortunate gentleman" who "wishes to fix himself in the house of some medical gentleman, who will have courage to refuse him any laudanum." Gillman had no intention of welcoming a drug addict into his home, but, like the man who thought Coleridge was picking his pocket and ended up paying for his library membership, he rapidly changed his mind, finding himself, on meeting the unfortunate gentleman, "spell-bound, without desire of release." And a good thing, too, since Coleridge, who asked to move in for a few weeks, stayed until his death eighteen years later.

Gillman never entirely weaned him off laudanum, but managed, by a combination of sympathy and guile, to control the doses. For the first time in his life, Coleridge felt no need to escape. He called Gillman and his wife "my most dear Friends," accompanied them on seaside vacations, and even, to show his gratitude, collaborated with Gillman on *An Essay on Scrofula*. During his years with the Gillmans, he wrote a few good poems and some memorable prose. He also gave a well-attended last lecture, which he described in a sardonic letter as being delivered by "a rare Subject—rather fat indeed—but remarkable as a fine specimen of a broken Heart."

His heart had been broken, he told a friend, by "four griping and grasping Sorrows": his failed marriage, his quarrels with Wordsworth, his thwarted love for Asra, and the ruin of his son Hartley. The last of these sorrows colored Coleridge's last years with an excruciating sense of déjà vu, as if Silas Tomkyn Comberbache had been revived in a drama whose tragedy had intensified and whose comedy had been entirely lost. Hartley was Coleridge's oldest and most brilliant child. Like his father, he was a prodigious scholar, a captivating talker, a daydreamer, and a drunk. In 1819, when Hartley was elected a fellow at Oxford, Coleridge was beside himself with joy. In 1820, when Hartley was dismissed for "sottishness, a love of low company, and general inattention to college rules," Coleridge was, in Mrs. Gillman's words, "convulsed with agony." During the week that followed, Dr.

Gillman stood watch by his bed in order to awaken him from screaming nightmares.

On a Saturday afternoon two years later, when Coleridge and Hartley were walking in London together, Hartley asked for some money to repay a debt. He pocketed the bills and agreed to rejoin his father no later than 6:00 P.M. Coleridge, filled with a terrible foreboding, cried, "Hartley! — Six!" As his son vanished wordlessly into the crowd, Coleridge found himself weeping so hard he could barely see. He later recalled the hours between six and midnight, during which he waited and Hartley never came, as "a Suffering which, do what I will, I cannot helping thinking of & being *affrightened by*, as a terror of itself, a self-subsisting separate Something. . . . O my God!" Coleridge lived twelve years beyond "THAT SATURDAY Evening," but the two runaways, one overwhelmed by his disgrace and the other overwhelmed by his loss, never saw each other again.

Hartley Coleridge—who went on to be a failed schoolmaster, a failed journalist, and the author of a small body of melancholy sonnets—is the "Dear Babe, that sleepest cradled by my side" in "Frost at Midnight," the first Coleridge poem I ever read. At sixteen, I knew nothing of either man's life. I could not guess that Coleridge, the tender father who vowed to show his firstborn son the "lovely shapes and sounds intelligible" of the natural world, would flee his wife and children; I could not guess that the "babe so beautiful" would grow up to flee his father. Now I know that domestic happiness was just another of Coleridge's misfired schemes. But biography can be false even when it is true. When I lose myself in the poem—the one form of escapism that never made its author feel guilty—the window of the little cottage, overhung with "silent icicles," still opens to a vista of infinite possibility.

MAIL

ome years ago, my parents lived at the top of a
steep hill. In his study, my father kept a pair of
binoculars with which, like a pirate captain
hoisting his spyglass to scan the horizon for treasure
ships, he periodically inspected the mailbox to check the
position of the flag. When the mail finally arrived, he
trudged down the driveway and opened the extra-large
black metal box, purchased by my mother in the same ac-
commodating spirit with which some wives buy their
husbands extra-large trousers. The day's load—a mountain of letters and about twenty pounds of review books
packed in Jiffy bags, a few of which had been pierced by
their angular contents and were leaking what my father
called "mouse dirt"—was always tightly wedged. But he
was a persistent man, and after a brief show of resistance
the mail would surrender, to be carried up the hill in a
tight clinch and dumped onto a gigantic desk. Until that
moment, my father's day had not truly begun.

His desk was made of steel, weighed more than a

refrigerator, and bristled with bookshelves and secret drawers and sliding panels and a niche for a cedar-lined humidor. (He believed that cigar-smoking and mail-reading were natural partners, like oysters and Mus-cadet.) Several books were written on that desk, but its finest hours were devoted to sorting the mail. My father hated Sundays and holidays because there was nothing new to spread on it. Vacations were taxing, the equivalent of forced relocations to places without food. His home-comings were always followed by daylong orgies of mail-opening—feast after famine—at the end of which all the letters were answered; all the bills were paid; the outgo-ing envelopes were affixed with stamps from a brass dis-penser heavy enough to break your toe; the books and manuscripts were neatly stacked; and the empty Jiffy bags were stuffed into an enormous copper wastebasket, cheering confirmation that the process of postal digestion was complete.

"One of my unfailing minor pleasures may seem dull to more energetic souls: opening the mail," he once wrote.

Living in an advanced industrial civilization is a kind of near-conquest over the unexpected. . . . Such efficiency is of course admirable. It does not, however, by its very nature afford scope to that perverse human trait, still not quite eliminated, which is pleased by the accidental. Thus to many tame citizens like me the morning mail functions as the voice of the unpredictable and keeps alive for a few minutes a day the keen sense of the unplanned and the un-plannable.

What unplanned and unplannable windfalls might the day's yield contain? My brother asked him, when he was in his nineties, what kinds of mail he liked best. "In my youth," he replied, "a love letter. In middle age, a job offer. Today, a check." (That was false cynicism, I think. His favorite letters were from his friends.) Whatever it was, it never came soon enough. Why were deliveries so few and so late (he frequently grumbled), when, had he lived in central London in the late seventeenth century, he could have received his mail ten or twelve times a day?

We get what we need. In 1680, London had mail service nearly every hour because there were no telephones. If you wished to invite someone to tea in the afternoon, you could send him a letter in the morning and receive his reply before he showed up at your doorstep. Postage was one penny.

If you wished to send a letter to another town, however, delivery was less reliable and postage was gauged on a scale of staggering complexity. By the mid-1830s,

> the postage on a single letter delivered within eight miles of the office where it was posted was . . . twopence, the lowest rate beyond that limit being fourpence. Beyond fifteen miles it became fivepence; after which it rose a penny at a time, but by irregular augmentation, to one shilling, the charge for three hundred miles. . . . There was as a general rule an additional charge of a half-penny on a letter crossing the Scotch border; while letters to or from Ireland had

to bear, in addition, packet rates, and rates for crossing the
bridges over the Conway and the Menai.

So wrote Rowland Hill, the greatest postal reformer in
history, who in 1837 devised a scheme to reduce and stan-
dardize postal rates and to shift the burden of payment
from the addressee to the sender.

Until a few years ago, I had no idea that before the
Victorian era, if you sent a letter out of town—and if you
weren't a nobleman, a member of Parliament, or some
other VIP who had been granted the privilege of free
postal franking—the postage was paid by the recipient.
This dawned on me when I was reading a biography of
Charles Lamb, whose employer, the East India House, allowed clerks to receive letters gratis until 1817: a substantial perk, sort of like being able to receive your friends'
calls on your office's 800 number. (Lamb, who practiced
stringent economies, also wrote much of his personal correspondence on company stationery. His most famous
letter to Wordsworth—the one in which he refers to
Coleridge as "an Archangel a little damaged"—is inscribed on a page whose heading reads "Please to state
the Weights and Amounts of the following Lots.")

Sir Walter Scott liked to tell the story of how he had
once had to pay "five pounds odd" in order to receive a
package from a young New York lady he had never met.
It contained an atrocious play called *The Cherokee
Lovers,* accompanied by a request to read it, correct it,
write a prologue, and secure a producer. Two weeks later,
another large package arrived for which he was charged a

similar amount. "Conceive my horror," he told his friend
Lord Melville, "when out jumped the same identical
tragedy of *The Cherokee Lovers,* with a second epistle
from the authoress, stating that, as the winds had been
boisterous, she feared the vessel entrusted with her former communication might have foundered, and therefore judged it prudent to forward a duplicate." Lord
Melville doubtless found this tale hilarious, but Rowland
Hill would have been appalled. He had grown up poor,
and, as Christopher Browne notes in *Getting the Message,*
his splendid history of the British postal system, "Hill
had never forgotten his mother's anxiety when a letter
with a high postal duty was delivered, nor the time when
she sent him out to sell a bag of clothes to raise 3*s* for a
batch of letters."

Hill was a born Utilitarian who, at the age of twelve,
had been so frustrated by the irregularity of the bell at
the school where his father was principal that he had
instituted a precisely timed campanological schedule.
Thirty years later, he published a report called "Post Office Reform: Its Importance and Practicability." Why, he
argued, should legions of accountants be employed to
figure out the byzantine postal charges? Why should
Britain's extortionate postal rates persist when France's
revenues had risen, thanks to higher mail volume, after
its rates were lowered? Why should postmen waste precious time waiting for absent addressees to come home
and pay up? A national Penny Post was the answer, with
postage paid by the senders, "using a bit of paper . . . covered at the back with a glutinous wash, which the

bringer might, by the application of a little moisture, attach to the back of the letter."

After much debate, Parliament passed a postal reform act in 1839. On January 10, 1840, Hill wrote in his diary, "Penny Postage extended to the whole kingdom this day! . . . I guess that the number despatched to-night will not be less than 100,000, or more than three times what it was this day twelve-months. If less I shall be disappointed." On January 11, he wrote, "The number of letters despatched exceeded all expectation. It was 112,000, of which all but 13,000 or 14,000 were prepaid." On May 6, the Post Office introduced the Penny Black, a gummed rectangle, printed with lampblack in linseed oil, that bore the profile of Queen Victoria: the first postage stamp. (Some historians—a small, blasphemous minority—confer that honor on a prepaid paper wrapper, inscribed with the date of transit, introduced in 1653 by Jean-Jacques Renouard de Villayer, the proprietor of a private postal service in Paris. But his wrapper wasn't sticky and it wasn't canceled, and thus, in my opinion, it bears the same relation to a stamp as a mud pie to a Sacher torte. In any case, Villayer's plan failed because practical jokers put mice in his postboxes and the mail got chewed.) The British press, pondering the process of cancellation, fretted about the "untoward disfiguration of the royal person," but Victoria became an enthusiastic philatelist who waived the royal franking privilege for the pleasure of walking to the local post office from Balmoral Castle to stock up on stamps and gossip with the postmaster. When Rowland Hill—by that time, *Sir* Rowland Hill—retired as Post Office Secretary in 1864, a *Punch* cartoon was captioned, "Should ROWLAND HILL have a statue? Certainly, if OLIVER CROMWELL should. For one is celebrated for cutting off the head of a bad King, and the other for sticking on the head of a good Queen."

The Penny Post, wrote Harriet Martineau, "will do more for the circulation of ideas, for the fostering of domestic affections, for the humanizing of the mass generally, than any other single measure that our national wit can devise." It was incontrovertible proof, in an age that embraced progress on all fronts ("every mechanical art, every manufacture, every thing that promotes the convenience of life," as Macaulay put it in a typical gush of national pride), that the British were the most civilized people on earth. Ancient Syrian runners, Chinese carrier pigeons, Persian post riders, Egyptian papyrus bearers, Greek *hemerodromes*, Hebrew dromedary riders, Roman equestrian relays, medieval monk-messengers, Catalan *troters*, international couriers of the House of Thurn and Taxis, American mail wagons—what could these all have been leading up to, like an ever-ascending staircase, but the Victorian postal system?

And yet (to raise a subversive question), might it be possible that, whatever the benefit in efficiency, there may have been a literary cost associated with the conversion from payment by addressee to payment by sender? If you knew that your recipient would have to bear the cost of your letter, wouldn't courtesy motivate you to write an extra good one? On the other hand, if you paid for it yourself, wouldn't you be more likely to feel you could get away with "Having a great time, wish you were here"?

I used to think my father's attachment to the mail was strange. I now feel exactly the way he did. I live in a five-story loft building and, with or without binoculars, I cannot see my mailbox, one of thirteen dinky aluminum cells bolted to the lobby wall. The mail usually comes around four in the afternoon (proving that the postal staircase that reached its highest point with Rowland Hill has been descending ever since), which means that at around three, *just in case,* I'm likely to visit the lobby for the first of several reconnaissance trips. There's no flag, but over the years my fingers have become so postally sensitive that I can tell if the box is full by giving it the slightest of pats. If there's a hint of convexity—it's very subtle, nothing as obvious, let us say, as the bulge of a tuna-fish can that might harbor botulism—I whip out my key with the same eagerness with which my father set forth down his driveway.

There the resemblance ends. The excitement of the treasure hunt is followed all too quickly by the glum realization that the box contains only four kinds of mail: 1) junk; 2) bills; 3) work; and 4) letters that I will read with enjoyment, place in a folder labeled "To Answer," and leave there for a geologic interval. The longer they languish, the more I despair of my ability to live up to the escalating challenge of their response. It is a truism of epistolary psychology that a Christmas thank-you note written on December 26 can say any old thing, but if you wait until February, you are convinced that nothing less than *Middlemarch* will do.

In the fall of 1998 I finally gave in and signed up for e-mail. I had resisted for a long time. My husband and I were proud of our retrograde status. Not only did we lack a modem, but we didn't own a car, a microwave, a Cuisinart, an electric can opener, a CD player, or a cell phone. It's hard to give up that sort of backward image. I worried that our friends wouldn't have enough to make fun of. I also worried that learning how to use e-mail would be like learning how to program our VCR, an unsuccessful project that had confirmed what excellent judgment we had shown in not purchasing a car, etc.

As millions of people had discovered before me, e-mail was fast. Sixteenth-century correspondents used to write "Haste, haste, haste, for lyfe, for lyfe, haste!" on their most urgent letters; my "server," a word that conjured up a luxurious sycophancy, treated *every* message as if someone's life depended on it. It got there instantly, caromed in a series of digital cyberpackets through the nodes of the Internet and restored to its original form by its recipient's 56,000-bit-per-second modem. (I do not understand a word of what I just wrote, but that is immaterial. Could the average Victorian have diagrammed the mail-coach route from Swansea to Tunbridge Wells?) More important, I *answered* e-mail fast—sometimes within seconds of its arrival. No more guilt! I used to think I didn't like writing letters. I now realize that what

I didn't like was folding the paper, sealing the envelope, looking up the address, licking the stamp, getting in the elevator, crossing the street, and dropping the letter in the postbox.

At first I made plenty of mistakes. I clicked on the wrong icons, my attachments didn't stick, and, not yet having learned how to file addresses, I sent an X-rated message to my husband (I thought) at gcolt@aol.com instead of georgecolt@aol.com. I hope Gerald or Gertrude found it flattering. But the learning curve was as steep as my parents' driveway, and pretty soon I was batting out fifteen or twenty e-mails in the time it had once taken me to avoid answering a single letter. My box was nearly always full—no waiting, no binoculars, no convexity checks, no tugging. I began to look forward every morning to the perky green arrow with which AT&T Worldnet beckoned me into my father's realm of the unplanned and the unplannable. What fresh servings of spam awaited me? Would I be invited to superboost my manhood, regrow my thinning hair, cleanse my intestines with blue-green algae, bulletproof my tires, say no to pain, work at home in my underwear, share the fortune of a highly placed Nigerian petroleum official, obtain a diploma based on my life experience from a prestigious nonaccredited university, or win a Pentium III 500 MHz computer (presumably in order to receive such messages even faster)? Or would I find a satisfying little clutch of friendly notes whose responses could occupy me until I awoke sufficiently to tackle something that required intelligence? As Hemingway wrote to Fitzgerald, describing the act of letter-writing: "Such a swell way to keep from working and yet feel you've done something."

My computer, without visible distension, managed to store a flood tide of mail that in nonvirtual form would have silted up my office to the ceiling. This was admirable. And when I wished to commune with my friend Charlie, who lives in Taipei, not only could I disregard the thirteen-hour time difference, but I was billed the same amount as if I had dialed his old telephone number on East Twenty-second Street. The German critic Bernhard Siegert has observed that the breakthrough concept behind Rowland Hill's Penny Post was "to think of all Great Britain as a single city, that is, no longer to give a moment's thought to what had been dear to Western discourse on the nature of the letter from the beginning: the idea of distance." E-mail is a modern Penny Post: the world is a single city with a single postal rate.

Alas, our Penny Post, like Hill's, comes at a price. If the transfer of postal charges from sender to recipient was the first great demotivator in the art of letter-writing, e-mail was the second. "It now seems a good bet," Adam Gopnik has written, "that in two hundred years people will be reading someone's collected e-mail the way we read Edmund Wilson's diaries or Pepys's letters." That may be true—but will what they read be any good? E-mails are brief. (One doesn't blather; an overlong message might induce carpal tunnel syndrome in the recipient from excessive pressure on the DOWN arrow.) They are also—at least the ones I receive—frequently devoid of capitalization, minimally punctuated, and creatively spelled. E-mail's greatest strength—speed—is also its Achilles' heel. In effect, it's always December 26. You are not expected to write *Middlemarch*, and therefore you don't.

In a letter to his friend William Unwin, written on August 6, 1780, William Cowper noted that "a Letter may be written upon any thing or Nothing." This observation is supported by the index of *The Faber Book of Letters, 1578–1939*. Let us examine the first few entries from the *d* section:

damnation, 87
dances and entertainments, 33, 48, 59, 97, 111, 275
death, letters written before, 9, 76, 84, 95, 122, 132, 135, 146,
        175, 195, 199, 213, 218, 219, 235, 237, 238, 259, 279
death, of children, 31, 41, 100, 153
dentistry, 220
depressive illness, 81, 87
Dictionary of the English Language, Johnson's, 61
Diggers, 22
dolphins, methods of cooking, 37

I have never received an e-mail on any of these topics. Instead, I am informed that Your browser is not Y2K-compliant. Your son left his Pokémon turtle under our sofa. Your essay is 23 lines too long.

Important pieces of news, but, as Lytton Strachey (one of the all-time great letter writers) pointed out, "No good letter was ever written to convey information, or to please its recipient: it may achieve both these results incidentally; but its fundamental purpose is to express the personality of its writer." *But wait!* you pipe up. *Someone just e-mailed me a joke!* So she did, but wasn't the personality of the sender slightly muffled by the fact that she forwarded it from an e-mail *she* received and sent it to thirty-seven additional addressees?

I also take a dim, or perhaps a buffaloed, view of electronic slang. Perhaps I should view it as a linguistic milestone, as historic as the evolution of Cockney rhyming slang in the 1840s. But will the future generations who pry open our hard drives be stirred by the eloquence of the e-acronyms recommended by a Web site on "netiquette"?

BTDT	been there done that
FC	fingers crossed
IITYWTMWYBMAD	if I tell you what this means will you buy me a drink?
MTE	my thoughts exactly
ROTFL	rolling on the floor laughing
RTFM	read the fucking manual
TANSTAAFL	there ain't no such thing as a free lunch
TAH	take a hint
TTFN	ta ta for now

Or by the "emoticons," otherwise known as "smileys"— punctional images, read sideways—that "help readers interpret the e-mail writer's attitude and tone"?

:-)	ha ha
:-(	boo hoo

(-:	I am left-handed
:-&	I am tongue-tied
%-)	I have been staring at this screen for 15 hours straight
{:-)	I wear a toupee
:-[	I am a vampire
:-F	I am a bucktoothed vampire with one tooth missing
=|:-)=	I am Abraham Lincoln
*:o)	I am Bozo the Clown

"We are of a different race from the Greeks, to whom beauty was everything," boasted a character in an 1855 novel by Elizabeth Gaskell. "Our glory and our beauty arise out of our inward strength, which makes us victorious over material resistance." We have achieved a similar victory of efficiency over beauty. The posthorn, a handsome brass instrument that once announced the arrival of mail coaches and made a cameo appearance in the sixth movement of Mozart's *Posthorn Serenade*, has been supplanted by an irritating voice that chirps, "You've got mail!" I wouldn't give up e-mail if you paid me, but I'd feel a pang of regret if the epistolary novels of the future were to revolve around such messages as

Subject: R U Kidding?
From: Clarissa Harlowe <claha@virtue.com>
To: Robert Lovelace <lovelaceandlovegirlz@vice.com>

hi bob, TAH. if u think im gonna run off w/ u, :-F. do u really think im that kind of girl?? if your looking 4 a trollop, CLICK HERE NOW: http://www.hotpix.com. TTFN.

I own a letter written by Robert Falcon Scott, the polar explorer, to G. T. Temple, Esq., who helped procure the footgear for Scott's first Antarctic expedition. The date is February 26, 1901. The envelope and octavo stationery have black borders because Queen Victoria had died the previous month. The paper is yellowed, the handwriting is messy, and the stamp bears the Queen's profile—and the denomination ONE PENNY. I bought the letter many years ago because, unlike a Cuisinart, which would have cost about the same, it was something I believed I could not live without. I could never feel that way about an e-mail.

I also own my father's old copper wastebasket, which now holds my own empty Jiffy bags. Several times a day I use his heavy brass stamp dispenser; it is tarnished and dinged, but still capable of unspooling its contents with a singular smoothness. And my file cabinets hold hundreds of his letters, the earliest written in his sixties in small, crabbed handwriting, the last in his nineties, after he lost much of his sight, penned with a Magic Marker in huge capital letters. I hope my children will find them some-day, as Hart Crane once found his grandmother's love letters in the attic,

> *pressed so long*
> *Into a corner of the roof*
> *That they are brown and soft,*
> *And liable to melt as snow.*

MOVING

From time to time, after we decided to move from New York City to western Massachusetts, my mind came to rest on the dispiriting example of James Montgomery Whitmore, my great-great-grandfather. Whitmore was a Mormon convert who traveled by covered wagon from Waxahachie, Texas, to Salt Lake City in 1857. Five years later, believing he had received a divine call to serve as a missionary along the Utah-Arizona border, he sold his mercantile business, hauled his family down to Pipe Spring, bought livestock, planted grapevines, and started spreading the word. In 1866, a band of Paiute Indians stole a flock of sheep from his pasture, and when Whitmore and a companion followed their tracks onto the open plain, they were ambushed and shot. A posse of ninety men found their bodies twelve days later, buried under the snow.

Though the chances of ambush in western Massachusetts were slim, I did not feel my family history augured well. My great-great-grandfather should have stayed in

Waxahachie; maybe we should stay in New York. But every time I walked past my husband's desk, I saw a yellow Post-it stuck to his bulletin board on which he had copied a quotation from Elaine May: "The only safe thing is to take a chance."

I'd lived in Manhattan for twenty-five years, George for twenty-one. We liked Mets games and New York accents. We liked Juilliard students who played Boccherini in subway stations and Sikh taxi drivers who wore turbans. We liked to walk from our loft in SoHo to Goody's, our favorite restaurant in Chinatown, and slurp Shanghai soup dumplings from large porcelain spoons. We liked our building, a turn-of-the-century box factory whose upper floors, when I moved there in 1978, were still served by a freight elevator that bore a hand-lettered sign: WE KNOW YOU ARE OLD AND FORGETFUL, BUT PLEASE RETURN THIS ELEVATOR TO THE GLUING DEPARTMENT.

In spite of all that, as we reached middle age we found ourselves inclining tropistically toward open spaces. It was impossible to describe our nature-cravings without sounding like Wordsworth, only more blubbery, so George and I avoided the subject around our friends, most of whom would have become seriously ill had they moved more than five blocks from the nearest bagel shop. We had both spent our early childhoods in New England, imprinted at tender ages by the smell of mown grass, the pea-green color of the air before a summer cloudburst, the taste of butter-and-sugar corn—the methods of whose eating my family had divided into two categories, Rotary (round and round) and Typewriter (left to right). (George and I added a third, Dot Matrix, for those who favor a back-and-forth approach.) We wanted those things again. Besides, our younger child was fond of projectiles—balls, slingshots, airplanes, rockets, arrows, torpedoes—and we were tired of shouting *"Not at the wedding pictures!"* Henry needed a yard.

We couldn't afford a weekend country house, and might not have wanted one anyway: too much like having a wife and a mistress. Serial monogamy seemed preferable. About ten years ago, we started talking about a second, rural phase. Since we were both writers, we could live anywhere we could plug in our modems. Cautiously, easing into the water by slow degrees, we visited college towns (bookstores, foreign films, possible teaching jobs) in Connecticut, Massachusetts, Vermont, and Maine. Some had houses priced beyond our means; some were too far from George's parents, who live in Boston. We settled on the Pioneer Valley of Massachusetts, named for the Puritan frontiersmen of the late seventeenth and early eighteenth centuries, large numbers of whom, like my great-great-grandfather, were massacred by Indians who thought they should have stayed home.

When Sir Walter Elliot, the self-absorbed baronet in *Persuasion*, becomes "distressed for money," he decides to move out of his ancestral manor in Somersetshire. It is suggested that he might be able to stay put if he practiced certain economies, but he cannot imagine such a fall. "What! Every comfort of life knocked off! Journeys, London, servants, horses, table,—contractions and restrictions every where. To live no longer with the decencies of a private gentleman! No, he would sooner quit Kellynch-hall at once, than remain in it on such disgraceful terms."

Sir Walter is defined by his home. *The Baronetage,* the only book he ever reads, opens of its own accord to the page headed "ELLIOT OF KELLYNCH-HALL." When he becomes ELLIOT OF A-RENTED-HOUSE-IN-BATH, will he still be himself? (Yes, says Jane Austen. He's just as obnoxious as ever.) It makes Sir Walter uneasy to think of a tenant living in *his* bedchamber, taking walks through *his* grounds. "I am not fond," he observes, "of the idea of my shrubberies being always approachable."

We felt that way, too. Afraid to burn our bridges, we decided to rent out our loft, furnished, so we could creep back if we started missing soup dumplings too severely. We owned no shrubberies, but I wasn't sure that I wished strangers to approach the corner of the living room where we had exchanged our wedding vows, the bathtub that had soothed my first labor pains, the bed in which we had exchanged a thousand embraces and a thousand confidences. Would they appreciate "Nudes for Nudes," a series of four pencil sketches by George's mother that we had mounted on the shower wall? (I have always believed that it is unsporting for fully clothed people to look at pictures of naked ones. The placement of this work was designed to even things up.) Would they be properly

impressed by the dining-room lamp, a large black contraption that had formerly graced the Erie Lackawanna
railway station in Hoboken, New Jersey, and was still
equipped with an anti-moth-immolation grille?

Sir Walter forbids anyone to mention that he is letting
his house: "It was only on the supposition of his being
spontaneously solicited by some most unexceptionable
applicant, on his own terms, and as a great favor, that he
would let it at all." We had no such qualms. We engaged
a real estate agent who dressed in black and had an Italian first name and a last name that was half French and
half Spanish. (It was hyphenated. Paolo was far too upscale to have only one name.) He walked around the loft.
I'm not sure he appreciated "Nudes for Nudes." I saw
him eyeing the aquamarine felt-tip-pen stain on the
chair near the front door, the grungy sofa, the ancient gas
stove. "It will be just right," he said in his expensive Italian-French-Spanish accent, "for a very special person."

Paolo wrote a display ad for the *New York Times*
real estate section headlined "EXPRESS YOUR INTERIOR
WORLD." At first I wasn't sure what this meant, but I
hadn't spent all those undergraduate hours on *explication
de texte* for nothing. Eventually I deconstructed it. It
meant: "You—the very special person whose next address will be 150 Thompson Street—may look like an investment banker, but inside your three-piece suit there
lives a starving poet who is crying to get out." The ad
continued: "This bohemian loft [read: there are no Sub-
Zero appliances] oozes charm & character [read: there are
children's fingerprints on the walls] only found in origi-

nal old SoHo [read: there's only one bathroom]." In its favor, the loft did have "wd flrs, orig beamed ceils, and grt
clsts."

Although there are pages and pages in *Persuasion*
about whether Sir Walter will find the right tenants,
there is not a word about cleaning up Kellynch-hall
before its prospective occupants come to inspect it.
Nineteenth-century novels never mention such matters.
The servants take care of them. Even if the tenants were
to drop in unannounced, the silver would already be pol-
ished, the floors waxed, the carpets beaten, and the ancestral portraits straightened. Paolo did not find our loft in a
similar state of readiness.

"The animals will have to go," he observed. The animals! How thrilling! He made it sound as if we kept a
pack of ocelots. In fact, our menagerie consisted of Silkie,
Susannah's hamster, and Bunky, Henry's frog, both of
whom lived in plastic boxes on the dining-room table,
underneath the lamp from the Erie Lackawanna railway
station.

"The kitchen is cluttered," he added. Before Paolo's arrival, I had spent three hours de-cluttering it. There wasn't
a single object on the counters. No one could toast, blend,
or make coffee in this kitchen; it was apparently owned by
people who had been born without digestive tracts. This
met with Paolo's approval. The problem was the family
photographs posted with magnets on the refrigerator. "No
personal effects," he explained, using a phrase I had heard
only on television detective shows, describing corpses that
had been robbed before they were murdered.

We banished the animals to Henry's bedroom, expunged our personal effects, spread a patchwork quilt on the sofa, replaced the Revere Ware teakettle with an imported red enamel coffeepot you couldn't pick up without a potholder, replaced the potholder, repainted the kitchen cabinets, scrubbed the windows, mopped the floors, rolled out a Persian rug the children weren't allowed to walk on, moved nine bags of toys to our neighbor's loft, and propped the pillows vertically on our bed, which meant that all the comfortable ones—the soft, saggy blobs you could bury your cheek in—were extradited to the closet. It could have been worse. If we'd been selling the loft instead of just renting it, we might have been tempted to hire a fluffer. (*Fluffer* is a term borrowed from pornographic filmmaking; he or she gets the male star ready for the camera.) In the housing market, the fluffer—also known as a stager—induces a temporary state of real-estate tumescence by removing much of what the client owns and replacing it, from a private warehouse of props, with new furniture, carpets, plants, paintings, towels, sheets, shower curtains, throw pillows, lamp shades, ice buckets (to hold champagne next to the Jacuzzi), breakfast trays (to hold tea and the Sunday *Times*), and Scrabble sets (to spell out BEAUTIFUL HOME). One fluffer ordered his client to remove a Georgia O'Keeffe painting from the wall and hide it under the bed. The colors were wrong.

Even though our loft was prepared by amateurs— self-fluffed, as it were—it had never looked better. We rented it to a kindly macroeconomist. The Elliots rent

Kellynch-hall to a kindly admiral who keeps the house shipshape, though he moves the umbrellas from the butler's room to the hallway and strips Sir Walter's dressing room of most of its looking glasses. "Oh Lord!" Admiral Croft explains, "there was no getting away from oneself."

"No getting away from oneself": that is both the fear and the hope of people who move. If you're pulling up stakes in order to remake your life and your character, what if you go to all that trouble and end up no more changed than Sir Walter? On the other hand, what if your identity is stuck with such firm adhesive to your old home that you leave little bits behind, and your new self is tattered and diminished?

According to the sociologist James M. Jasper, it is no wonder that Americans name their cars Quests and Explorers and Ventures and Caravans. We move more than anyone else. In a typical year, one in five Americans relocates, whereas in Japan it's one in ten, in Britain one in twelve, and in Germany one in twenty-five. Each of those one in five Americans flouts the law laid down by almost every book whose plot revolves around relocation: *Stay where you are!* Can you think of a happy book about moving? I can't. It's fine to hie yourself to Troy or Oz or Narnia or Wonderland, as long as you end up back where you started—and, indeed, a frequent theme in stories about travel, whether real or imaginary, is the central character's strenuous efforts to get home. (Traveling is always thought to be more enjoyable than moving: we envy foreign correspondents but pity army brats.) A typical children's-book move is the one made by the orphaned heroines of *The Secret Garden* and *A Little Princess* from warm, fecund India to cold, dreary England. Even the *Little House* series, in which the Ingalls family stays intact and reasonably content as it moves from woods to prairie to creek to lake, becomes incrementally less idyllic with each volume. Most discouraging of all is the sort of educational volume, illustrated with photographs of cheerful moving men, that extols the joys of leaving your friends and starting a new school. You can tell the author is lying because the next title in the series is usually something like *Tonsillectomies Are Fun!*

And as we pass out of childhood, what do we read? *Martin Chuzzlewit*, in which young Martin moves to America, falls ill with fever, and loses all his money in a land swindle; *Main Street*, in which Carol Kennicott moves to Gopher Prairie and is suffocated by small-town provincialism; *The Grapes of Wrath*, in which the Joads move to California and—well, you know the rest. From birth to adulthood, our lives are a journey away from Eden. And that, because it matches our own trajectory, is the only direction the literary moving van can go.

When I was eight, our family moved from Connecticut to California. The weather was balmy, the beaches broad, the incidence of runny noses low. But objective merit means little to a child. All I knew was that the light was too bright, the shadows too hard, the landscape too brown.

I hoped that the move to Massachusetts would be not a deracination but a reracination. During our last three months in New York, I was encouraged in this view by the e-mails I received from the owner of the place we were going to rent, a foursquare yellow clapboard farm-house built in 1804, on the east bank of the Connccticut River, by Elijah and Resign Graves. (Those Puritans! It was coercive enough to name your daughter Felicity or Chastity, but Resign!) Our landlord, whose family was planning to spend a sabbatical year in London, was a sci-ence writer who had just completed the labels for an in-sect exhibition that featured a rare birdwing butterfly collected by a man who was eaten by cannibals. As the spring and summer progressed she sent us frequent na-ture bulletins: The trillium was blooming. Two orioles had been spotted on the quince bushes. The red fox had trotted through the pasture. The hummingbirds had re-turned. The mother wrens were peering out of their nest box. Her boys had found two toads.

How familiar it all sounded! Frances Hodgson Bur-nett would never have sent Sara Crewe back to India, but our lives were not a novel. Might it be possible to journey backward instead of forward?

We'd find out soon enough. But first we had to deal with our To Do list: Fill out change-of-address forms. Reglue kitchen cabinet knobs. Fix toilet. Unclog bathtub drain. Get sofa and chairs cleaned. Go to dentist. Get renter's insurance. Disconnect phone and utilities. Send transcripts to children's new school. Switch bank accounts. Duplicate keys. Write farewell note to neighbors. Cancel *New York Times*. We had to compile a list of instructions for our tenants: Put out garbage on Monday, Wednesday, and Friday, recycling on Wednesday only. Open hall closet by pushing, not pulling. Remember to replace water in plastic lint catcher. (Our future landlord wrote us a similar list: Don't let children touch bat poop in attic. Protect potato chips from mice by suspending bags from ceiling. Feed suet to woodpeckers and thistle seed to finches.)

Our grt clsts held layers we hadn't seen for years. New Yorkers, lacking attics and basements and garages, treat their closets like trash compactors (or, to put it more charitably, like the squeezing machines that turn duck breasts into *canard pressé*). The by-products of our shared lives had been squished into a dense sediment that, when pried out and spread on the floor, expanded by a factor of ten. How could we have accumulated so many outgrown hiking boots, so many mateless mittens, so many letters from people who had once loomed large and now, like distant trees, had shrunk to near-invisibility?

I had imagined that our final weeks would be sweet, a last hurrah of city-love, but we were too busy for sentiment. In our early days together, George and I had walked down Prince Street every night, holding hands. Now we walked the same route every afternoon, dragging our cast-off possessions to Goodwill.

We packed 347 boxes. (I know the number because it is written on the moving company's invoice. The total

weight was six tons.) We vowed we would never buy another book. We broke our nails peeling packing tape from
slippery brown rolls. We kept losing our scissors, our
Magic Markers, our color-coded dots (green for the new
house, red for storage). Later, we discovered that we had
boxed them up.

When we left for Massachusetts, I had been awake for
three days and three nights. Our rented car was so full
that the rearview mirror was useless. Susannah held
Silkie's terrarium between her knees. I held Bunky's
aquarium between my feet. As we drove north on Inter-
state 91, I thought: This is the worst mistake I have ever
made in my life. George and I will never get another
writing assignment. Susannah will hang out at the mall.
Henry will chew gum. The sushi will be frozen.

When I was younger, I spent several years studying the
Hmong, a mountain people whose entire culture had
evolved around their frequent migrations. Their wood
and bamboo houses could be taken apart, portaged in
modular chunks, and put back together. Their great arts
were textiles, jewelry, music, and storytelling. Everything
was physically and psychologically portable, so it was possible to move without cutting off one's roots.

In the car, I was certain we could never do that: our
reassembled lives would look nothing like our old ones.
But when we drove down our new driveway, my despair
lifted with a whoosh that cannot be explained even by
the lability of fatigue. The yellow house was beautiful. A

few minutes later, the moving van pulled in, and I asked
the driver to locate a box that I had labeled on all six
sides: BALLS BALLS BALLS BALLS BALLS BALLS. At a
school auction, we had been the high bidders on a set of
balls of every conceivable genre—football, basketball,
volleyball, softball, tennis, soccer, bocce. Henry spilled
them out onto the back lawn and ran in circles, tossing
and kicking and rolling.

That night, as we lay in bed, I murmured, "George!
We're really in the country! Listen to the peepers on the
riverbank!"

"Those aren't peepers on the riverbank," George said
gently. "That's Bunky, on Henry's bureau. We're hearing
him over the baby monitor."

As the weeks passed, we missed New York, sometimes
acutely, but that did not make us love the Pioneer Valley
any less. I reminded myself that the most happily remar-
ried widows are the ones who had the best first mar-
riages.

George and Susannah swam every day in the Connecticut River and reported what they had seen on the
bottom (a golf bag, a glove, a potato). Henry and I bicy-
cled to the corner store, which, unlike its SoHo analogue,
had signs in the window offering night crawlers and
chewing tobacco—but it also had seven brands of ice
cream and a luxuriant hawthorn tree out front. On our
fourth visit, Henry settled himself under the hawthorn
and said, with a five-year-old's easily acquired sense of
permanency, "This is where we always sit."

Last month, we signed the papers on an 1807 brick

farmhouse in a neighboring town. When we learned that it needed a new roof, we refused to look at any materials that were not guaranteed to last at least twenty-five years.

It is true that I had a great-great-grandfather who was killed by Indians, but these days I find myself thinking more often of another great-great-grandfather, also a Utah pioneer. John Sharp moved from Clackmannan-shire, Scotland, where he had worked in a coal mine, to New Orleans, then to St. Louis, and finally, in 1850, to Salt Lake City. His journey to Utah was, I will grudg-ingly admit, even more arduous than our journey up In-terstate 91. The first snows overtook his wagon train, and he and his party spent the winter in caves they dug in the side of Red Butte Canyon, roofing them with wagon boxes and walling them with stones.

After Sharp arrived in Salt Lake City, the skills he had acquired in the mines of Clackmannanshire won him the contract for quarrying and hauling, by ox-drawn wagon, the huge blocks of granite that were to form the foundation of the Mormon Temple. He became superin-tendent of the quarry, then a Mormon bishop, and finally a director of the Union Pacific Railroad. In 1869, at Promontory Point, he helped drive the golden spike that completed the transcontinental railroad, enabling people to move across the country by train instead of covered wagon.

In 1904, an article about John Sharp was published in

the monthly magazine of the Young Men's Mutual Improvement Association of the Church of Jesus Christ of
Latter-Day Saints. It pointed out that had Sharp stayed in
Scotland, he might never have left the coal pits. His life,
noted the anonymous author, "teaches the lesson that to
succeed one must struggle with circumstance, and overcome by faith and toil; that change, evolution, and action,
secure mental and material progress; while, on the contrary, traveling self-satisfied in ruts, seeking sameness,
and courting inaction, are conditions to be avoided."

A PIECE OF COTTON

When we bought an old farmhouse last summer in a small New England town, the elderly couple who had lived there for many years left us a set of plastic lawn chairs, a garbage can, a tool bench, a wheelbarrow, and an American flag. On September 13, two days after the attacks, we raised it, with our children's help, to half staff. Our six-year-old son enjoyed pulling the halyard; on its way up the peeling white-painted pole, next to the big maple tree in the front yard, the flag made an interesting and satisfying sound, partway between a squeak and a ring. We'd read up on half-masting protocol, which dictates raising the flag briskly to the peak and then slowly bringing it halfway down. George said, "This flag is lowered now, but it will rise again, just as our country will." It is useful to have children around at such times: they authorize clichés that their parents deeply believe but might otherwise hesitate to voice.

Neither George nor I had ever owned a flag, not even

a little one to wave on the Fourth of July. The closest George had come was the pair of stars-and-stripes bell-bottoms he had worn in the sixties (in violation of section 176d of the United States Flag Code: "The flag should never be used as wearing apparel, bedding, or drapery"). The closest I had come was the handkerchief-sized Whole Earth banner that I had knotted to the aerial of my brother's car in the fall of 1970, before we drove from our home in California to college in Massachusetts. We took the whole earth idea seriously: what a provincial notion, I remember thinking, to fly a flag that implied one was a citizen of only *part* of the earth!

If you had asked me then what it meant to be a flag owner—or, as I would have called it, a flag-waver, as if holding a flag in one's hand was inherently more ridiculous than stringing it up a pole—I would have said "Vietnam." (Silly question; everyone knew what it meant.) But my answer would have been false. My disdain for the flag wasn't political; it was social. When I burrow back into my seventeen-year-old self as thoroughly as the intervening decades allow, here's what I fear she was thinking: If you were a flag-waver, you lived in a split-level house with vinyl siding in a suburb of Omaha. You had a crew cut. Your children belonged to the 4-H Club and had a dog that, without irony—there was no irony within a five-hundred-mile radius of Omaha—they had named Fido. You read *Reader's Digest* and listened to Andy Williams. You ate tuna casserole and frozen peas for dinner, followed by lime Jell-O with little pieces of banana suspended in it. You had never traveled east of Wichita (or maybe west; I had never been to either Omaha or Wichita, and knew only that they were both somewhere in the amorphous middle of things). You had never heard of Herman Hesse.

"Sept. 11 made it safe for liberals to be patriots," the critic George Packer has written. Like me, Packer once considered flag-waving an embarrassing display of bad taste, though he associated it more with the working class than with the Cleaveresque middle class. Either way, it wasn't the sort of thing our families indulged in. When people like Packer and me were teenagers, we had little interest in the socioeconomic tiers that separated the upper middle class, to which we belonged, from what we might have called the "underprivileged class," a group with which we professed heartfelt solidarity, whether or not we'd ever met any of its members. And in those days, in those circles (which pretended to be egalitarian but were in fact unthinkingly, unapologetically, unbelievably snobbish), America was itself déclassé, a simpleminded concatenation of Uncle Sam and log cabins and Smokey the Bear. I mean, really: if you wanted a stimulating dinner companion, would you pick Betsy Ross or Jean-Paul Sartre?

In March of 1918, a year after the United States entered World War I, a mob surrounded a Montana man named E. V. Starr and tried to force him to kiss an American flag. Starr refused, saying, "What is this thing anyway? Nothing but a piece of cotton with a little paint on it and some other marks in the corner there. I will not kiss that thing. It might be covered with microbes."

The previous month, Montana had enacted a flag-desecration statute that became the model for the 1918 federal Sedition Act, outlawing "disloyal, profane, scurrilous, or abusive language" about the United States government or its flag. Starr was charged with sedition, fined $500, and sent to the state penitentiary for ten to twenty years of hard labor. Ruling on Starr's appeal, the federal district court judge who heard the appeal wrote:

> In the matter of his offense and sentence, obviously petitioner was more sinned against than sinning. . . . [The mob's] unlawful and disorderly conduct, not his just resistance, nor the trivial and innocuous retort into which they goaded him, was calculated to degrade the sacred banner and to bring it into contempt. Its members, not he, should have been punished.

Although he called the court that had sentenced Starr "stark, staring, raving mad"—no penalty that severe had ever been meted out, or would ever be meted out again, in a United States flag desecration case—the judge ruled that the state law was nonetheless constitutional and that he had no other choice than to uphold the conviction.

The unfortunate Starr's only bit of luck was that the Montana mob did not assault him, unlike the automobile workers in Lansing, Michigan, who, the same winter, after a fellow employee wiped his hands on a flag, had chopped a hole in the ice that covered the Grand River, tied a clothesline to the man's foot, and submerged him until he apologized; or the saloon patrons in Thermopolis, Wyoming, who, the previous year, had lynched a man for shouting "Hoch lebe der Kaiser." (In the latter case, the victim was cut down in the nick of time by the city marshal. The *Chicago Tribune* reported: "Revived with cold water, he was forced to kneel and kiss the American flag. He then was warned to get out of town. He did.")

I read about these cases—they are collected in a fascinating and disturbing book called *Desecrating the American Flag: Key Documents of the Controversy from the Civil War to 1995*, edited by Robert Justin Goldstein—while I was attending a conference in Colonial Williamsburg, the omphalos of Americana. It felt strange to underline E. V. Starr's question in a hotel room crammed with hooked rugs and embroidered samplers. What *is* this thing, anyway? I thought. Is it just a piece of cotton? Is it, as Katha Pollitt put it, explaining why she had refused her daughter's request to hang a flag in their window, a symbol of "jingoism and vengeance and war"? Or is it, as a group of New York women wrote in the dedication of a silk flag they had sewn for Union soldiers in 1861, "the emblem of all you have sworn to defend: / Of freedom and progress, with order combined, / The cause of the *Nation*, of *God*, and *Mankind*"?

In the weeks after September 11, I saw for the first time that the flag—along with all its red, white, and blue collateral relations—is what a semiotician would call "polysemous": it has multiple meanings. The flag held aloft by the pair of disheveled hitchhikers who squatted next to their backpacks on Route 116, a mile from our home, meant *We will not rape or murder you.* The red, white, and blue turban worn by the Sikh umbrella vendor a friend walked past in Dupont Circle, not far from the White House, meant *Looking like someone and thinking like him are not the same thing.* The flag on the lapel of a Massachusetts attorney mentioned in our local paper—on seeing it, his opposing counsel had whispered to a colleague, "I'm so screwed, do you have a flag pin I can borrow?"—meant *I am morally superior.* The flags brandished by two cowboy-hatted singers at a country fair we attended on the day the first bombs fell on Afghanistan meant *Let's kill the bastards.* The Old Glory bandanna around the neck of the well-groomed golden retriever I saw on a trip to Manhattan meant *Even if I have a Prada bag and my dog has a pedigree, I'm still a New Yorker and I have lost something.* The flag in our front yard meant *We are sad. And we're sorry we've never done this before.*

Newspapers printed full-page color flags for flagless readers to tape on their windows. NBC put stars and stripes on its peacock. The Macdougal Street Tattoo Company in Greenwich Village gave pro bono patriotic tattoos—something new under the sun—to nearly five hundred World Trade Center rescue workers. A Pennsylvania man had a flag shaved into his buzz cut. A New York restaurant called The Tonic introduced a dessert called Stars and Stripes: white mascarpone panna cotta encircled by red and blue pomegranate- and grape-flavored stars. The design of a new 34-cent flag stamp, captioned UNITED WE STAND, was rushed through several layers of U.S. Postal Service red tape in record time so that a billion stamps could be available by November 1. The space shuttle *Endeavor* carried more than six thousand flags to the International Space Station and brought them back for distribution to the families of those killed on September 11. Our son made a flag from a leaf and a twig to mark the final days of his vegetable garden and asked if he should fly it at half staff.

When I visited my mother in Florida, I paused at the window of the gift shop in the Fort Myers airport. Outside, a National Guardsman with an M-16 patrolled the corridor. Inside, on a bed of gold-flecked gauze, reposed the largest collection of red, white, and blue objects I had ever seen: flags, streamers, key chains, pens, fans, T-shirts, baseball caps, figurines, coffee mugs, beer steins, shot glasses, menorahs, postcards with photographs of flags surrounded by oranges and flamingos, bumper stickers that said THESE COLORS NEVER RUN, starfish that said GOD BLESS AMERICA. The meaning of these objects had nothing to do with terrorism; the flag was a "theme," like the "Underwater Theme" we'd chosen for our high school senior prom. ("Japan?" "Too hard to draw all those geishas." "Outer Space?" "Too much black and white." "Underwater?" "Now there's an idea.") I had recently seen a coffee-table book of flag-oriented antiques, each beautifully photographed and embellished with little airbrushed shadows, arranged on the pages like jewels in a Tiffany vitrine. *Patriotic Shield*

Pin Box. Uncle Sam Hat Brooch. Presidential Cigar Band.
Admiral Perry Whiskey Flask. Wheatlet Trading Card.
They all looked incredibly expensive, but what they
had gained in value over the years they had lost in meaning: they were no longer about patriotism in wartime,
they were about being collectible. The Fort Myers
gift shop window was indistinguishable from a page in
that book. It was already meaningless. All it needed was
a caption: "Americana—Assorted Ephemera & Folk
Art, 2001."

But just because most of the flag paraphernalia was
dreck didn't mean that all of it was. I was caught short by
the reproduction of Edward P. Moran's flag-filled 1886
painting *Statue of Liberty Enlightening the World,* placed
in *The New York Times* by the Museum of the City of
New York, accompanied by a quotation from Le Corbusier: "New York is not a completed city. . . . It is a city
in the process of becoming. Today it belongs to the world.
Without anyone expecting it, it has became the jewel in
the crown of universal cities. . . . New York is a great diamond, hard and dry, sparkling, triumphant!" Just typing
those words, nearly three months later, brings on the peculiar feeling of congestion I still feel every morning
when I read the obituaries in the *Times* and start thinking about the widow who gave birth to twins on September 15 or the woman who lost both a husband and a son. I
had lived in New York for twenty-five years, twenty-two
of them within walking distance of the World Trade
Center. The trauma center nearest the site was the hospital where our daughter was born; Engine 24/Ladder 5,

where Mayor Giuliani, covered in ash, set up his temporary command post, was our corner firehouse. I felt ashamed when I caught myself thinking of this as a neighborhood tragedy rather than a global one; it was the solipsistic fallacy of believing that the telephone pole you're closest to is taller than all the rest, just because it *looks* taller. Our Massachusetts friends said to us, "You must be so relieved to have moved!" And though we did feel relief, our feelings were complicated and contradictory. We loved New York all the more because of what had been done to it. George said it was like the upwelling of tenderness one might feel upon hearing that an old lover had been grievously injured. I knew, though it seemed like a shamefully trivial emotion, that one of the reasons Moran and Le Corbusier affected me was homesickness.

It was good to see George watching the World Series one night. Until then, we had been unable to watch any television programs that did not deal with September 11. Flying above center field at Yankee Stadium was a torn flag. It was shaped like an oriflamme, the banner the king's army carried in twelfth-century France, split at one end with flying edges like two flames. The flag, which had flown somewhere inside the World Trade Center, had been found in the rubble and nearly disposed of (Flag Code section 176k: "The flag, when it is in such condition that it is no longer a fitting emblem for display, should be destroyed in a dignified way, preferably by burning"). The Port Authority intervened, and Sergeant Antonio Scannella, a police officer who had lost thirteen of his squad's eighteen members, became the flag's unofficial caretaker, saying, "You can't throw an American flag in the garbage." When Max von Essen, the son of the New York City fire commissioner, sang "The Star-Spangled Banner" (the only national anthem I can think of that is explicitly about a flag), my throat surprised me by catching.

Why did the lopsided flag that billowed across our television screen pull strings that had previously been unpullable? I think it moved me *because* it was damaged, like the city itself. A clean rectangle whose proportions conform precisely to the executive order issued in 1912 by President Taft—hoist (height) 1.0, fly (length) 1.9, hoist of union (blue field) .5385, fly of union .76, width of each stripe .0769, diameter of each star .0616—calls up less passionate associations than, for instance, the flag flown by the 16th Connecticut Volunteer Regiment in the Civil War. When surrender was inevitable, the soldiers tore the flag into fragments to keep it from falling into enemy hands. A historian named F. C. Hicks wrote in 1926:

> The regiment, some five hundred strong, was sent to a prison camp where most of the men remained until the close of the war. Each piece of the colors was sacredly preserved. When a soldier died his piece was entrusted to a comrade. At the end of the war the weary prisoners returned to their homes, each bringing his bit of star or stripe with him. All these torn fragments were patched together and the regimental colors, nearly complete, are now preserved in the State House at Hartford.

To read about our nation's vexillological history—"vexil-lology," the study of flags, is an excellent crossword-puzzle word that derives from the Latin *vexillum*, or banner—is to experience a series of bitter disillusionments. Betsy Ross did not design the Stars and Stripes; she sewed flags for the navy in the spring of 1777, but there is no evidence that the flag as we know it was conceived before June 14 of that year, when the Continental Congress, which had pre-viously been more concerned about designing a national seal, finally got around to the flag: "RESOLVED: that the flag of the United States be made of thirteen stripes, al-ternate red and white; that the union be thirteen stars, white in a blue field, representing a new constellation." (Many historians now attribute the circular shape of that constellation to Francis Hopkinson, a delegate from New Jersey, though late-eighteenth-century flags show the stars disposed in a variety of arrangements, including a single vertical line and an X.) George Washington did not cross the Delaware with flag in hand; the Battle of Trenton was fought six months before the Flag Resolu-tion. The flag's design did not immediately engrave it-self on the memories of all who beheld it; in 1778, Benjamin Franklin and John Adams informed the King of the Two Sicilies that the stripes were "alternately red, white, and blue," and on a ceramic jug manufactured in Liverpool at about the same time, an American ship flew a flag with blue and yellow stripes. "The Star-Spangled Banner" did not immediately become the national an-them; though it was written by Francis Scott Key during the Battle of Fort McHenry in 1814 (and set to the tune of "To Anacreon in Heaven," a British drinking song celebrating a bibulous Greek poet who is said to have choked to death on a grape), it was not officially adopted until 1931.

In fact, as Scot M. Guenter explains in *The American Flag, 1777–1924: Cultural Shifts from Creation to Codification*, it was not until Rebel forces fired on the flag at Fort Sumter on April 12, 1861, that the flag, which earlier had been used mainly for identifying naval and commercial vessels, was transformed into a symbol men were willing to die for. If it took the Civil War to sacralize the flag—as the historian George Henry Preble wrote in 1880, "its prose became poetry"—it took the commercialism of the ensuing decades to turn its poetry back into prose. In 1905, an anti-desecration circular lamented the use of the flag in advertisements for "bicycles, bock beer, whiskey, fine cambric, bone knoll, sour mash, tar soap, American pepsin chewing gum, theatres, tobacco, Japan tea, awnings, breweries, cigars, charity balls, cuff buttons, dime museums, floor mats, fireworks, furriers, living pictures, picnic grounds, patent medicines, poolrooms, prize fights, restaurants, roof gardens, real estate agencies, sample rooms, shoe stores, soap makers, saloons, shooting galleries, tent makers, variety shows, [and] vendors of lemon acid." Tame stuff, perhaps, compared with David Bowie, his face painted red, white, and blue and a miniature vodka bottle resting on his naked clavicle (caption: "Absolut Bowie"), or with the nightmarish ads that clog the Internet ("Render this Osama Voo-Doo doll completely Pin-Laden! 6-inch doll for a Stocking Stuffer

Price of $9.99! Comes with 6 red, white, and blue extra-sharp Patriot Pins").

In 1989, the School of the Art Institute of Chicago mounted an exhibit called "What Is the Proper Way to Display the American Flag?" In order to reach the leather-bound ledger in which they were asked to record their responses, viewers had to walk on a flag laid on the floor. "For days," reported *The Detroit News*, "veterans picked the flag up off the floor, folded it in the ceremonial military fashion and placed it on the shelf. Their faces were almost always stoic; one was visibly in tears at the sight of grimy footprints on the flag. Moments later, however, the flag was unfolded by supporters of the art, usually students with indignant faces, who shook out the flag like a bedsheet, and then draped it on the floor."

The same year, in a controversial case called *Texas v. Johnson*, Supreme Court Justice Anthony Kennedy explained why he had concluded, with great reluctance, that flag-burning is a form of free speech and therefore protected by the First Amendment. "Though symbols often are what we ourselves make of them," he wrote, "the flag is constant in expressing beliefs Americans share, beliefs in law and peace and that freedom which sustains the human spirit. The case here today forces recognition of the costs to which those beliefs commit us. It is poignant but fundamental that the flag protects those who hold it in contempt."

We kept our flag at half staff longer than President Bush decreed that we should, and then, after raising it to full staff, we continued to fly it after most of our neighbors had put theirs away. Maybe we were making up for lost time. Maybe we needed to see our flag flying in order to convince ourselves that even though anti-Muslim protesters marching near a mosque in Bridgeview, Illinois, had waved flags and chanted "U.S.A.! U.S.A.!," we could choose another meaning in Whately, Massachusetts: the one a Chicago flag committee had in mind in 1895 when it called the Stars and Stripes "our greater self."

I had not looked closely at our flag when we raised it, so I decided to take it down one day to see whether it was made of cotton or silk. It was a raw afternoon in early December; freezing rain was falling on gray patches of snow. Section 174c of the Flag Code prohibits display in inclement weather, but a handful of local diehards were still flying their flags rain or shine, twenty-four hours a day, so we had followed suit. The flag was sodden and looked like a shrouded bat. When I lowered it and detached the grommets from the halyard, I could see that it was made of nylon. Black letters printed on the hoist, so faded I could barely make them out, read DURA LITE. The red stitching that connected the stripes was beginning to bleed. The embroidered white stars were fraying. As I refastened the brass clip, I tried hard to keep the old, wet, shabby flag from touching the ground.

THE ARCTIC HEDONIST

mong the many mental games with which my insomniac father whiled away the small hours of the night, his favorite was called I Shook Hands with Shakespeare. He had shaken hands with the actress Cornelia Otis Skinner, who had in turn presumably shaken hands with her father, Otis Skinner. *He* had shaken hands with Edwin Booth . . . and so on, down through Junius Brutus Booth, Edmund Kean, David Garrick, Thomas Betterton, Sir William D'Avenant, and Richard Burbage. Finally, as dawn crept through the blinds, William Shakespeare extended his hand. (My father admitted a shaky manual link between Kean, who was born in 1787, and Garrick, who died in 1779.)

I myself have shaken hands with the arctic explorer Vilhjalmur Stefansson. Our degrees of separation number only two. Aware of my febrile interest in the history of polar exploration, my father once mentioned that, many years earlier, he had been introduced to Stefansson.

"*Stefansson?*" I panted. "What was he like?"

"The only thing I recall," said my father, "is his unfortunate smell."

I didn't hold this against Stefansson; it was part and parcel of being an explorer. (One of his expeditionary companions once noted that "he considers any attention to cleanliness, hygiene and camp sanitation as 'military fads.'") In any case, through Stefansson (or, in some cases, through people *he* met), I have also clasped hands with Robert Peary, Matthew Henson, Fridtjof Nansen, Roald Amundsen, Robert Falcon Scott, and Ernest Shackleton—the men who dominated the great period of arctic and antarctic exploration between 1880 and the First World War. I have spent many nights establishing these bonds (*Let's see ... Stefansson must have met Amundsen in 1906, when they were both at Herschel Island; Amundsen visited Nansen in Norway in 1900—or was it 1899?*), and, like my father, discovered that the handshaking game is far better at keeping one awake than at putting one to sleep.

The closest hand was the best; it still felt warm. For more than twenty years, I have therefore considered Vilhjalmur Stefansson "my explorer." During the course of three expeditions between 1906 and 1918, my explorer was the first white man to visit the Copper Inuit of Victoria Island; traveled twenty thousand miles by dogsled; discovered the world's last major landmasses, a series of islands in the Canadian archipelago; and set what a colleague called "the world's record for continuous Polar service" (five and a half years, an interval Stefansson considered nothing to boast about, since many of his

Inuit friends had lived in the Arctic without apparent difficulty for more than eight decades).

What most endeared Stefansson to me was his conviction that the far north was not meant to be endured; it
was meant to be enjoyed. If you knew what you were doing, you could have a "bully time" up there. His favorite
temperature was −40°. (Temperatures below −50° were
manageable but not quite so bully, since they required
you to breathe through your mouth. "Your nose," he observed, "is less likely to freeze when there is cold air
merely outside of it instead of both inside and out.")
When he was above 66° north latitude, he insisted that
his spirits were jollier, his appetite keener, and his wavy
blond hair thicker. His most famous book, a 784-page account of his third expedition, was called *The Friendly
Arctic*.

The Friendly Arctic? In 1921, when it was published,
Macmillan might as well have brought out a book called
The Friendly Pit Viper. The previous century had seen a
series of arctic catastrophes, from Sir John Franklin's
1845 expedition in search of the Northwest Passage (130
dead of scurvy, starvation, and lead poisoning), to George
Washington De Long's 1879 attempt to reach the North
Pole from Siberia (twenty dead of exposure, starvation,
and drowning), to Adolphus Greely's 1881 expedition to
Ellesmere Island (nineteen dead of exposure, starvation,
and drowning). It was true that in 1909 Robert Peary
reached the North Pole—or claimed he did—but he

would have had a more comfortable journey had he not
lost eight of his toes to frostbite on an earlier expedition.

The Friendly Arctic was an in-your-face title, and
that's why Stefansson chose it. After all, he wrote, everyone knows what the Arctic is like:

> The land up there is all covered with eternal ice; there is
> everlasting winter with intense cold; and the corollary of
> the everlastingness of the winter is the absence of summer
> and the lack of vegetation. The country, whether land or
> sea, is a lifeless waste of eternal silence. The stars look
> down with a cruel glitter, and the depressing effect of the
> winter darkness upon the spirit of man is heavy beyond
> words. On the fringes of this desolation live the Eskimos,
> the filthiest and most benighted people on earth, pushed
> there by more powerful nations farther south, and eking
> out a miserable existence amidst hardship.

Wrong, wrong, wrong, wrong. Eternally icy? Montana,
Stefansson explained, in the tone a parent might use to
drum something obvious into the skull of an unusually
dim-witted child, is far colder; arctic summers are hot;
there are 762 species of arctic flowering plants. Silent? In
the summer, the tundra resounds with the squawks of
ducks, the cackles of geese, the cries of plovers, the
screams of loons, and the howls of wolves (which, when
heard on starlit nights, constitute "the most romantic sort
of music"). Once the ice starts to freeze against the coast,

> there is a high-pitched screeching as one cake slides over
> the other, like the thousand-times magnified creaking of a
> rusty hinge. There is the crashing when cakes as big as a

church wall, after being tilted on edge, finally pass beyond
their equilibrium and topple down upon the ice; and when
extensive floes, perhaps six or more feet in thickness, gradually bend under the resistless pressure of the pack until
they buckle up and snap, there is a groaning as of super-
giants in torment and a booming which at a distance of a
mile or two sounds like a cannonade.

Depressing? According to Stefansson, "an Eskimo laughs
as much in a month as the average white man does in a
year." A benighted people? The Inuit are honest, consid-
erate, courteous, hospitable, fun-loving, self-sufficient,
and morally superior to any but the "rarest and best of
our race."

In other words, the Arctic was not (as Peary had described it, using the sort of language to which readers
had become accustomed) "a trackless, colorless, inhos-
pitable desert"; it was a high-latitude Arcadia. Precipita-
tion was light. Gale-force winds were rare. Water was
abundant, even at sea, since salt leaches out of ice floes
within a few seasons, rendering them deliciously fresh.
Illness was infrequent; tuberculosis was seldom transmit-
ted during the winter because "the spit is likely to freeze
when it is voided." And the region flowed, if not with
milk and honey, then with caribou, polar bear, walrus,
and seal, all there for the taking (even if shooting seals
beneath the polar ice "resembles hunting as we commonly think of it less than it does prospecting"). Why
burden your sledges with heavy provisions, thereby limit-
ing an expedition's duration and range, when, if you
merely did what the Inuit had been doing for centuries,

you could live off the land? "Do not let worry over to-morrow's breakfast interfere with your appetite at din-ner," Stefansson liked to tell his men. "The friendly Arctic will provide."

If the Arctic was so friendly, it followed that you didn't need to be a masochist in order to explore it. Stefansson had nothing but contempt for "heroes who conquered the Frozen North," since he considered the Frozen North a myth and the metaphor of battle entirely wrongheaded. (Friends don't fight.) He believed this sort of bunkum had been invented to satisfy readers in over-stuffed armchairs who found narratives of ease and pleasure less riveting than hyperbolic accounts of "suf-fering, heroic perseverance against formidable odds, and tragedy either actual or narrowly averted." Stefansson's stance—partly a pose, but only partly—was that being an arctic explorer was no harder than any other job. He wrote to a friend that the prospect of returning to the far north was as pleasant as, and not much different from, the prospect of spending a winter in Heidelberg. Finding your way to a remote Inuit camp was "no more wonder-ful than knowing that a fifteen-minute walk will take you to the Flatiron Building from the Washington Arch." Why pretend you were bristling with machismo when living in the Arctic was a piece of cake?

I recognized the Stefansson shtick just last week when I was reading a German fairy tale to my seven-year-old son. Its plot revolved around a king who assigns progres-

sively more impossible tasks to a cocksure young man
—stealing a dragon's flying horse, stealing the dragon's
blanket, and finally stealing the dragon himself. The
penalty for failure is death by dismemberment. Every
time the king ups the ante, our hero says, "Is that all?
That is easily done." In fairy tales, such characters are
never punished for their bravado; they always perform
their assigned tasks without breaking a sweat and end up
marrying the king's daughter. In this case, the young
man not only follows the prescribed formula for success
but has the pleasure of watching the dragon eat the king
for dinner.

The voice of that young man is the same voice Tom
Wolfe had so much fun with in *The Right Stuff*, that of
the airline pilot who, as his plane seems about to crash,
drawls into the intercom:

> "Now, folks, uh . . . this is the captain . . . ummmm . . .
> We've got a little ol' red light up here on the control panel
> that's tryin' to tell us that the *land*in' gears're not . . . uh . . .
> *lock*in' into position when we lower 'em . . . Now . . . *I* don't
> believe that little ol' red light knows what it's *talk*in'
> about—I believe it's that little ol' red *light* that iddn'
> workin' right" . . . faint chuckle, long pause, as if to say, *I'm
> not even sure all this is really worth going into—still, it may
> amuse you* . . . "But . . . I guess to play it by the rules, we
> oughta *hum*or that little ol' light . . ."

You know that pilot will never have an elevated pulse,
never admit there's an emergency, and never crash the
plane.

I first encountered this attitude of studied insouciance thirty years ago, when I took a wilderness course at the National Outdoor Leadership School in Wyoming, during an era of outdoorsmanship considerably more primitive than the present one. Our catchphrase was "No prob." Five weeks without tents or stoves? No prob. We slept under tarps suspended from trees and lit fires twice a day, forcarming ourselves for rainy days by squirreling little bundles of dry sticks in our pockets—our six-foot-three-inch leader tenderly called them "twiggies," to underline how very cozy and unintimidating the whole venture was—just as Stefansson had squirreled handfuls of dry *Cassiope tetragona* (arctic heather) in *his* pockets. No fancy freeze-dried food? No prob. We baked bread, pizzas, even birthday cakes by heaping hot coals on our frying pan lids, and cleaned the blackened pans with swags of limber pine, which we called Wind River Brillo. No food at all during the five-day "survival expedition" at the end of the course? No prob. We fished for trout and foraged for grouse whortleberries. Those five days were the hungriest of my life, but I wouldn't have dreamed of admitting it. (Stefansson: "Any traveler who complains about going three or four days without food will get scant sympathy from me.") That dragon was *easy* to steal.

A few years later, when I became an instructor at NOLS, the ratio of bluster to genuine joie de vivre declined precipitously. We pooh-poohed Outward Bound, our competitor in the wilderness-skills field, as unnecessarily anhedonic. OB promised to build character by asking its disciples to face fear and hardship; NOLS asked, as

Stefansson had, "What fear? What hardship?" One winter we took out a group of mountaineering students for a couple of weeks to climb Wind River Peak on skis. It was ten below zero, but we built both a small igloo and a gigantic snow cave, in whose toasty precincts we threw off most of our clothes and stretched as luxuriously as cats next to a radiator. At night, when we schussed the snowfields above Deep Creek Lakes, the hoarfrost reflected the full moon, and it was almost as bright as day.

That was small stuff, and very long ago. But, years later, it was enough to make me understand what Stefansson meant when he described hunting caribou on Banks Island on a cold, clear day: "In his exuberance of good health it is difficult for the arctic hunter to feel anything but pleasure in almost any kind of weather or almost any circumstance. I suppose what I am trying to explain is about what the Biblical writer had in mind when he spoke of a strong man rejoicing to run a race."

Stefansson had just the sort of upbringing you'd expect: pioneer-style, in a one-room cabin in the Dakota Territory, with scant food but plenty of Norse sagas recited in the evening by his Icelandic parents, who had emigrated first to Manitoba and then to the United States. When he was eighteen, he set himself up as a winter grazier, caring for the livestock of local farmers. The great blizzard of 1897 hit during his first season, and all his assistants quit, unwilling to work on skis or shovel their way into barns buried in snowdrifts. No prob. Stefansson carried on alone and, of course (because the young man in the fairy tale never labors in vain), didn't lose a single head of cattle.

At the University of North Dakota, Stefansson was thrown out of his boardinghouse for espousing Darwinism and then expelled from college for spotty attendance and "a spirit of insubordination." (His fellow students staged a mock funeral. His hearse was a wheelbarrow, his widow a black-clad classmate whose tears were facilitated by an onion wrapped in a handkerchief.) No prob. After finishing up at the University of Iowa and attending graduate school at Harvard, where he switched his field from divinity to anthropology, he was offered the post of ethnologist on the 1906 Anglo-American Polar Expedition to northwest Canada. He and his expedition never ended up intersecting, since he traveled overland to the Mackenzie Delta—solo, of course—and the ship that carried his colleagues failed to penetrate the ice beyond Point Barrow, two hundred miles to the west. No prob. He spent the winter living with the Inuit, collecting ethnographic artifacts, learning Inuktitut, and formulating his belief that the only way to get along in the Arctic was to dress and hunt and eat like a local. "I was gradually being broken in to native ways," he wrote.

By the middle of October, I had thrown away my nearly outworn woollen suit and was fur clad from head to heel, an Eskimo to the skin. I never regretted the lack of a single item of such arctic clothing as money can buy in America

or Europe. . . . A reasonably healthy body is all the equip-
ment a white man needs for a comfortable winter among
the arctic Eskimos.

Two more expeditions followed, one primarily ethnographic, the other geographic and scientific. By the end
of his tenth arctic winter, Stefansson was the uncontested
master of what he called "polarcraft," a body of knowledge he later codified in a volume called the *Arctic Manual*. Although it was commissioned by the U.S. Army as a
survival guide for Air Corps fliers who were forced to
make emergency landings in the far north, its author
couldn't resist transforming it into a how-to book on
what *he* liked to do—live off the land, with minimal provisions, for years at a time. (A downed flier, for instance,
would be unlikely to make use of his observation that the
ideal sled dog is bred by crossing a husky or a malamute
with a wolf.)

The *Arctic Manual* is my favorite Stefansson book.
The chances that I will ever need to apply its lessons may
be slender. But just as devotees of Martha Stewart feel
more secure knowing they *could* make a wedding center-
piece from belt buckles and gumdrops, even if they never
actually have to, so I derive a certain degree of comfort
from reading and rereading Stefansson's arctic tips. It re-
assures me to know that pussy willow fuzz can be used for
the wick of a seal-oil lamp. That two lemon-sized chunks
of iron pyrite, struck together, will start a fire faster than
matches. That it is possible to cook with the hair and
wool of a musk ox or grizzly bear, one hide being suffi-

cient for two or three eight-quart pots. That if you are not ashore during the spring thaw, you should select a thick floe on which to spend the summer, and resume your travel in the fall. That a dead seal can be easily dragged, but a polar bear tends to flip upside down. That you should not rub decayed caribou brains on your clothes, since the hides will stiffen. That skin boats can be boiled and eaten. That the best way to approach a seal you wish to shoot is to look like a seal yourself: wear dark clothing, wriggle along the ice, and occasionally flex your legs from the knees as if scratching lice with your hind flippers.

It is important to understand that these pieces of advice are offered in a spirit not of grit-teethed stoicism—*I may be facing death, but, by God, at least I know enough not to rub decayed caribou brains on my clothes*—but of casual bonhomie, as if the author and the reader were in perfect agreement that this stuff is *fun*. Stefansson wasn't a survivor; he was a voluptuary. Why would anyone wish to wear wool when "nothing feels so good against the skin—not even silk—as underwear of the skin of a young caribou"? Why live in a house when an igloo, lit with a single candle, resembles "a hemisphere of diamonds"? Why employ Inuit or Indians to do one's hunting when one could have the satisfaction of doing it oneself? "I would as soon think of engaging a valet to play my golf," he observed, "or of going to the theatre by proxy."

Stefansson admitted that his hunting had not always been fruitful. In lean times he had eaten snowshoe lashings, sealskins intended for boot soles, and the remains of a bowhead whale that had been beached for four years. (It tasted like felt.) But when the Arctic chose to show its friendly aspect, its cuisine practically made him swoon. Frozen raw polar bear meat had the consistency of raw oysters; half frozen, it was more like ice cream. The soft, sweet ends of mammal, bird, and fish bones were scrumptious. Seal-blood soup, an especial favorite, warranted a recipe that might have intrigued Brillat-Savarin:

> When the meat has been sufficiently cooked it is removed from the pot which is still hanging over the fire. Blood is then poured slowly into the boiling broth with brisk stirring the while. In winter small chunks of frozen blood dropped in one after the other take the place of the liquid blood poured in summer. . . . The consistency of the prepared dish should be about that of "English pea soup."

The *ne plus ultra* of arctic fare was caribou flesh: in ascending order of "gustatory delight," the brisket, ribs, and vertebrae; the tongue; the head, especially the fat behind the eyes; the little lump of fat near the patella of the hind leg; and the marrow of the bones near the hoof, which was customarily rolled into little balls and eaten raw. Stefansson maintained that a high-fat, all-meat diet not only pleased the palate but also cured depression, prevented scurvy, reduced tooth decay, and relieved constipation. (When he was in his late forties and living in New York City, he undertook to prove his nutritional theories by spending a year, under the supervision of Bellevue Hospital, on an exclusively carnivorous diet. Not only did he remain healthy, but he was proud to report that X-rays revealed an "unusual . . . absence of gas from the intestinal tract during the meat-eating period.")

Given the abundance of northern pleasures, it is not surprising that Stefansson envisioned a time when the Arctic would be viewed not as the end of the earth but as a vital crossroads. Musk oxen and reindeer would be domesticated for world consumption, "not for the exclusive delectation of wolves, wolverines, foxes and ravens." The skies would be filled with airplanes traveling the shortest routes between New York, London, Moscow, and Peking; the seas would be filled with submarines. In his book *The Northward Course of Empire*, he reproduced a graph conceived by an American sociologist named S. Columb GilFillan. The horizontal axis was chronological, from 3400 B.C. to 2200 A.D. The vertical axis was meteorological. The great world centers were arrayed along this graph, with Upper Egypt (mean annual temperature 77°) succeeded by Athens (63°), Rome (59°), Constantinople (57°), London (50°), and Moscow (39°), among others. The implication was clear: if the trend continued, in a few hundred years the Arctic would be the nexus of civilization.

My Stefansson shelf grew over the years, augmented by birthday contributions from my husband. The books had been out of print for decades and had tissue-thin maps tucked in pockets at the back. They were all *by* Stefansson. It was only when I started work on this essay that I bought a half-dozen books *about* Stefansson. And that is where the probs began.

I learned that not everyone liked my explorer as much as I did. After Stefansson visited Australia on a lecture tour in 1925, a *Sydney Bulletin* reporter observed delicately that "our late visitor . . . is a many sided man. I would call him nothing less than an Hexagon, and he may even be an irregular crystal." Controversial during his lifetime (his peers thought him a publicity hound, his bosses thought him a troublesome maverick), the irregular crystal has attracted a new round of criticism in recent years—the same period of polar revisionism during which Peary was accused of fraud and Scott was exposed as a dangerous bumbler. The two most serious charges are that Stefansson abandoned his Inuit family and that, on his third expedition, he was responsible for the deaths of eleven men.

For two decades I had read Stefansson's laconic references to Fannie Pannigabluk, the widowed seamstress who accompanied him and his friend Natkusiak on his second expedition. It had never occurred to me that she was Stefansson's mistress; after all, he noted several times that every expedition required an Inuit seamstress to make and repair caribou-hide and sealskin clothing. Gísli Pálsson, an Icelandic anthropologist who has interviewed four of Stefansson's Inuit grandchildren, writes, "Pannigabluk was presented as primarily a domestic worker, with no formal recognition of her role as either spouse, partner, or key informant." Stefansson never publicly acknowledged the relationship or the son it produced; nor, apparently, did he provide financial support. It is true that Robert Peary and Matthew Henson also had sons by Inuit women and that both of them jettisoned their families in similar fashion. Peary went a step further and published a nude photograph of his mistress. But *Stefansson*? The man who wrote of the Inuit, "I cannot see how anyone who knows them can wish more for anything than that he was rich and could repay their kindness fully"?

The accusations that swirl around Stefansson's third expedition allege an even more serious abandonment. In July of 1913, the HMCS *Karluk* steamed out of Port Clarence, Alaska, en route to the Beaufort Sea, with Stefansson and half the members of the Canadian Arctic Expedition on board. (The rest were on two other ships, bound for scientific work in the Northwest Territories.) By mid-August, the *Karluk* was icebound. In mid-September, Stefansson, accompanied by three men from his scientific staff and two Inuit, left on a ten-day hunting trip to provision the ship with meat for the winter. Two days later, the sixty-mile-an-hour winds of the season's first blizzard dislodged the *Karluk*'s ice floe, and the ship drifted hundreds of miles to the west, far out of Stefansson's reach. The *Karluk* was eventually crushed in the ice, and most of its men made their way to Wrangel Island, north of Siberia. They suffered severe hardships there—starvation, snow blindness, frostbite, gangrene, and, in one case, the amputation of a toe with a pair of tin-cutting shears. Eleven died. Many years later, one of the survivors wrote: "Not all the horrors of the Western Front, not the rubble of Arras, nor the hell of Ypres, nor all the mud of Flanders leading to Passchendaele, could blot out the memories of that year in the Arctic."

It is indisputable that Stefansson left the ship. The question is whether he intended to return. In *The Ice Master: The Doomed 1913 Voyage of the* Karluk, Jennifer Niven argues that he did not: caribou were scarce in the area; he left his best hunters on board the *Karluk*; and— the most damning evidence—the ship's meteorologist believed that Stefansson, who, two days before he departed, had been observed reading the diaries from De Long's catastrophic 1879 expedition, left the ship "for fear of losing his life."

The Canadian historian Richard J. Diubaldo disagrees. In his scrupulously fair-minded biography *Stefansson and the Canadian Arctic,* he argues that "there is strong evidence to suggest that he wished he had never left." I share his view. If Stefansson had no intention of returning, why did he leave his chronometer and thirteen hundred dollars on board? Why did he leave detailed instructions on the flags and beacons that were to guide his return over the ice? Why didn't he take the best sledges? After the blizzard, why did he hasten west along the coast to Cape Smythe, if not to catch up with the *Karluk*?

I think Stefansson took off for ten days because he couldn't bear to be on board a ship that wasn't moving, couldn't bear to sit around playing bridge or listening to his men give concerts on the mandolin and harmonica. Stasis was poison to him. But whether or not he abandoned ship, I am now convinced that he is responsible for the deaths of his men. He assembled the expedition hastily, recruiting an inexperienced crew that included a drug addict who carried his hypodermic needles in a

pocket-sized case. He insisted on using a ship that had
been declared unsound by his captain. And though he
was one of the greatest solo operators in history, he was a
terrible leader. He had no idea how to organize large
groups of men or large amounts of cargo, and he had so
little regard for his staff and crew that, instead of welcoming them as soon as he arrived at the naval yard from
which the *Karluk* was to embark, he kept them waiting
while he held a five-hour press conference.

Worst of all was his cavalier attitude toward the men
he lost. His journal entry from August 11, 1915, when he
heard the news, disposes of their fate in two sentences far
less laden with emotion than the entry, four years earlier,
in which he mourned the death of his favorite sled dog.
He blamed his men for being less competent than he
would have been in their situation—in effect, for being
so foolish as to succumb to the myth of the Frozen North.
Did he fail to realize that *The Friendly Arctic* might not
be the most tasteful title for a book about an expedition
on which eleven people died?

The frontispiece of *The Friendly Arctic* is a black-and-
white photograph of Stefansson dragging a seal across
the ice. He is wearing mukluks and a caribou-skin parka.
Under his right arm he carries a rifle; under his left, a
harpoon. His head is bare, and he is alone.

He selected the picture while he was living at the
Harvard Club in New York City, beginning a career of
lecturing and writing that made him, in the words of one

biographer, "the equivalent of a senior officer who has become too valuable to go out on combat patrols, and must sit at his headquarters surrounded by his staff." He shelved his plan to camp on an ice floe with one or two companions, moving with the polar drift for a couple of years. Instead, from his desk, he organized abortive schemes to colonize Wrangel Island and breed reindeer on Baffin Island. He lived for forty-four years after he returned from his third expedition, and—because of illness, because his reputation in Canada had lost its luster, because he had traded his caribou-skin parka for a double-breasted suit—he never traveled in the Arctic again.

It is not as great a tragedy as the abandonment of one's family, not as great as the loss of eleven lives, but it is nonetheless a tragedy that when *The Friendly Arctic* appeared, the Macmillan Company could not include the same note it had inserted before the title page of *My Life with the Eskimo* in 1913:

NOTE TO THE FIRST EDITION

The publishers regret that owing to Mr. Stefansson's departure on his new expedition to the far North he was unable to read the final proofs of this volume.

COFFEE

hen I was a sophomore in college, I drank coffee nearly every evening with my friends Peter and Alex. Even though the coffee was canned; even though the milk was stolen from the dining hall and refrigerated on the windowsill of my friends' dormitory room, where it was diluted by snow and adulterated by soot; even though Alex's scuzzy one-burner hot plate looked as if it might electrocute us at any moment; and even though we washed our *batterie de cuisine* in the bathroom sink and let it air-dry on a pile of paper towels next to the toilet—even though Dunster F-13 was, in short, not exactly Escoffier's kitchen, we considered our nightly coffee ritual the very acme and pitch of elegance. And I think that in many ways we were right.

Alex came from Cambridge, but Peter was alluringly international. He had a Serbian father, an American mother, and a French coffeemaker. At my home in Los Angeles, the coffee-making process had taken about three seconds: you plunked a spoonful of Taster's Choice freeze-dried crystals in a cup, added hot water, and stirred. With Peter's *cafetière à piston*, you could easily squander a couple of hours on the business of assembling, heating, brewing, pouring, drinking, disassembling, and cleaning (not to mention talking), all the while telling yourself that you weren't really procrastinating, because as soon as you were fully caffeinated you would be able to study like a fiend. The *cafetière* had seven parts: a cylindrical glass beaker; a four-footed metal frame; a chrome lid impaled through its center by a plunger rod topped with a spherical black knob; and three metal filtration discs that screwed onto the tip of the plunger in a sequence for whose mastery our high SAT scores had somehow failed to equip us. After all the pieces were in place, you dolloped some ground coffee into the beaker, poured in boiling water, and waited precisely four minutes. (In the title sequence of *The Ipcress File*, special agent Harry Palmer unaccountably fails to carry out this crucial step. As an eagle-eyed critic for *The Guardian* once observed, Palmer grinds his beans and pops them into his *cafetière*, but *fails to let the grounds steep before he depresses the plunger*. How could any self-respecting spy face his daily docket of murder and mayhem fueled by such an anemic brew?) Only then did you apply the heel of your hand to the plunger knob and ram the grounds to the bottom of the beaker, though the potable portion always retained a subtle trace of Turkish sludge. What a satisfying operation! The plunger fit *exactly* into its glass tunnel, presenting a sensuous resistance when you urged it downward; if you pressed too fast, hot water and grounds would gush out the top. The whole process involved a good deal of screwing and unscrewing and trying not to make too much of a mess. Truth to tell, it was a lot like sex (another mystery into which I was initiated that year, though not by Peter or Alex), and as soon as you'd done it once, you wanted to do it again and again and again.

Disdaining the dining hall's white polystyrene cups, most of which had gone a little gray around the rim, each of us had procured our own china mug. Mine had a picture of a polka-dotted pig on it, an allusion to the frequency with which it was refilled. I stirred its contents with a silver demitasse spoon whose bowl was engraved with the name of my hometown. "Firenze" or "Cap d'Antibes" would have been preferable to "Los Angeles," but I did like the feel of the calligraphy against my tongue. Although the whole point of coffee-drinking was to be grown up—no Pepsi Cola for bohemian intellectuals like us!—the amount of milk and sugar with which we undermined our sophisticated brew suggested that we needed to regress as much as we yearned to evolve. The end product resembled melted coffee ice cream.

It was the last time in my life that coffee slowed the hours rather than speeding them up. Those long, lazy nights—snow falling outside on Cowperthwaite Street, the three of us huddled inside in a warm, bright room, talking of literature and politics until the rest of Dunster House was asleep—were an essential part of my college curriculum. After all, wasn't education a matter of infusing one's life with flavorful essences, pressing out the impurities, and leaving only a little sludge at the bottom?

It is said that around the seventh century, somewhere near the Red Sea—whether it was Ethiopia or Yemen is a subject of debate—a herd of goats ate the magenta berries of a shiny green shrub and began to act strangely. In a classic 1935 study called *Coffee: The Epic of a Commodity*, the German journalist Heinrich Eduard Jacob described their behavior thus:

> All night, for five nights in succession—nay, for seven or eight—they clambered over rocks, cutting capers, chasing one another, bleating fantastically. They turned their bearded heads hither and thither; with reddened eyes they gambolled convulsively when they caught sight of the goatherds, and then they darted off swift as arrows speeding from the bow.

Having observed the frisky goats, a local imam—a sort of medieval Carlos Castaneda—roasted the berries in a chafing dish, crushed them in a mortar, mixed them with boiling water, and drank the brew. When he lay down, he couldn't sleep. His heartbeat quickened, his limbs felt light, his mood became cheerful and alert. "He was not merely thinking," wrote Jacob. "His thoughts had become concretely visible. He watched them from the right side and from the left, from above and from below. They raced like a team of horses." The imam found that he could juggle a dozen ideas in the time it normally took to consider a single one. His visual acuity increased; in the glow of his oil lamp, the parchment on his table looked unusually lustrous and the robe that hung on a nearby peg seemed to swell with life. He felt strengthened, as Jacob put it, "by heavenly food brought to him by the angels of Paradise."

Whoa! Little did the hopped-up imam know that while he and the goats were happily tripping, 1,3,7-trimethylxanthine (otherwise known as caffeine) was coursing through their veins, stimulating brain activity by blocking the uptake of adenosine, a neurotransmitter that, if left to its own devices, makes people (and goats) sleepy and depressed. Just enough of the stuff and you feel you've been fed by the angels of Paradise; too much, and Mr. Coffee Nerves (a diabolical cartoon character with a twirly mustache who graced Postum ads in the 1930s) gets you in his grip.

Caffeine was first isolated in 1819, when the elderly Johann Wolfgang von Goethe, who had swallowed oceans of coffee in his younger days and regretted his intemperance, handed a box of Arabian mocha coffee beans to a chemist named Friedlieb Ferdinand Runge and enjoined him to analyze their contents. Runge extracted an alkaloid that, as Jacob put it, "presents itself in the form of shining, white, needle-shaped crystals, reminding us of swansdown and still more of snow." Caffeine is so toxic that laboratory technicians who handle it in its purified state wear masks and gloves. In *The World of Caffeine*, by Bennett Alan Weinberg and Bonnie K. Bealer, there is a photograph of the label from a jar of pharmaceutical-grade crystals. It reads in part:

WARNING! MAY BE HARMFUL IF INHALED OR SWALLOWED. HAS CAUSED MUTAGENIC AND REPRODUCTIVE EFFECTS IN LABORATORY ANIMALS. INHALATION CAUSES RAPID HEART RATE, EXCITEMENT, DIZZINESS, PAIN, COLLAPSE, HYPOTENSION, FEVER, SHORTNESS OF BREATH. MAY CAUSE HEADACHE, INSOMNIA, NAUSEA, VOMITING, STOMACH PAIN, COLLAPSE AND CONVULSIONS.

Anyone who doubts that caffeine is a drug should read some of the prose composed under its influence. Many of the books on coffee that currently crowd my desk share a certain . . . *velocity*, as if their authors, all terrifically buzzed at 3:00 A.M., couldn't get their words out fast enough and had to resort to italics, hyperbole, and sentences so long that by the time you get to the end you can't remember the beginning. (But that's only if you're uncaffeinated when you read them; if you've knocked back a couple of *cafés noirs* yourself, keeping pace is no sweat.) Heinrich Eduard Jacob boasts that his narrative was "given soul by a coffee-driven euphoria." Gregory Dicum and Nina Luttinger claim that while they were writing *The Coffee Book: Anatomy of an Industry from Crop to the Last Drop,* they

sucked down 83 double Americanos, 12 double espressos, 4 perfect ristrettos, 812 regular cups (from 241 French press-loads, plus 87 cups of drip coffee), 47 Turkish coffees, a half-dozen regrettable cups of flavored coffee, 10 pounds of organic coffee, 7 pounds of fair trade coffee, a quarter pound of chicory and a handful of hemp seeds as occasional adjuncts, 1 can of ground supermarket coffee (drunk mostly iced), 6 canned or bottled coffee drinks, 2 pints of coffee beer, a handful of mochas, 1 pint of coffee concentrate, a couple of cappuccinos, 1 espresso soda, and, just to see, a lone double tall low-fat soy orange decaf latte.

Their book contains only 196 pages and doesn't look as if it took very long to write; that decaf latte aside, the authors' caffeine quota per day must have been prodigious. (But note their exactitude: coffee makes you peppy, but it doesn't make you sloppy.)

The contemporary master of the genre is Stewart Lee Allen, known as "the Hunter S. Thompson of coffee journalism," whose gonzo masterwork, *The Devil's Cup*, entailed the consumption of "2,920 liters of percolated, drip, espresso, latte, cappuccino, macchiato, con panna, instant and americana." (It isn't very long, either. By the time Allen finished, his blood must have been largely composed of 1,3,7-trimethylxanthine.) Following the historical routes by which coffee spread around the globe, Allen gets wired in Harrar, San'a, Istanbul, Vienna, Munich, Paris, Rio de Janeiro, and various points across the United States, attempting to finance his travels and his coffee habit with complicated transactions involving forged passports and smuggled art. He ends up on Route 66, in search of the worst cup of coffee in America, in a Honda Accord driveaway filled with every form of caffeine he can think of: Stimu-Chew, Water Joe, Krank, hi-caf candy, and a vial of caffeine crystals (scored from an Internet site that features images of twitching eyeballs) whose resemblance to cocaine occasions some exciting psychopharmacological plot twists when a state trooper pulls him over in Athens, Tennessee.

But in the realm of twitching eyeballs, even Stewart Lee Allen can't hold a candle to Honoré de Balzac, the model for every espresso-swilling writer who has followed in his jittery footsteps. What hashish was to Baudelaire, opium to Coleridge, cocaine to Robert Louis Stevenson, nitrous oxide to Robert Southey, mescaline to Aldous Huxley, and Benzedrine to Jack Kerouac, caffeine was to Balzac. The habit started early. Like a preppie with an expensive connection, he ran up alarming debts with a concierge who, for a price, was willing to sneak contraband coffee beans into Balzac's boarding school. As an adult, grinding out novels eighteen hours a day while listening for the rap of creditors at the door, Balzac observed the addict's classic regimen, boosting his doses as his tolerance mounted. First he drank one cup a day, then a few cups, then many cups, then forty cups. Finally, by using less and less water, he increased the concentration of each fix until he was eating dry coffee grounds: "a horrible, rather brutal method," he wrote, "that I recommend only to men of excessive vigor, men with thick black hair and skin covered with liver spots, men with big square hands and legs shaped like bowling pins." Although the recipe was hell on the stomach, it dispatched caffeine to the brain with exquisite efficiency.

From that moment on, everything becomes agitated. Ideas quick-march into motion like battalions of a grand army to

its legendary fighting ground, and the battle rages. Memories charge in, bright flags on high; the cavalry of metaphor
deploys with a magnificent gallop; the artillery of logic
rushes up with clattering wagons and cartridges; on imagination's orders, sharpshooters sight and fire; forms and
shapes and characters rear up; the paper is spread with ink.

Could that passage have been written on decaf?

Balzac's coffeepot is displayed at 47 rue Raynouard in
Paris, where he lived for much of his miserable last
decade, writing *La Cousine Bette* and *Le Cousin Pons*, losing his health, and escaping bill collectors through a secret door. My friend Adam (who likes his espresso strong
but with sugar) visited the house a few years ago. "The
coffeepot is red and white china," he wrote me, "and
bears Balzac's monogram. It's an elegant, neat little
thing, almost nautical in appearance. I can imagine it
reigning serenely over the otherwise-general squalor of
his later life, a small pharos of caffeine amid the gloom."

When I was fifteen, I went to Paris myself. I didn't realize it at the time, but that summer I stood at a fateful
crossroads. One way led to coffee, the other to liquor.

I was a student on a high school French program in
an era when the construction of *in loco parentis* was considerably looser than it is now. I began each day with a
café au lait at a local patisserie and ended it with a *crème
de menthe frappé* at a bar. One afternoon, after we had
left Paris and were traveling through southern France,
the director of the program invited me to lunch at a

three-star restaurant in Vienne, where we shared *pâté de foie gras en brioche, mousse de truite Périgueux, turbot à la crème aux herbes, pintadeau aux herbes, gratin dauphinois, fromages, gâteau aux marrons, petits fours,* and a Brut Crémant '62. I'd never drunk half a bottle of wine before. Afterward, en route to Avignon in Monsieur Cosnard's Mercedes, I was asked to help navigate, a task that appeared inexplicably difficult until I realized I was holding the map upside down.

The conclusion was clear: *Why would anyone want to feel like this?* Although I never became a teetotaler, I knew—especially when I woke up the next morning with a hangover—that I would cast my lot with caffeine, not with alcohol. Why would I wish my senses to be dulled when they could be sharpened? Why would I wish to mumble when I could scintillate? Why would I wish to forget when I could remember? Of course, since even in those days I was a loquacious workaholic who liked to stay up late, you might think I'd pick a drug that would nudge me closer to the center of the bell curve instead of pushing me farther out on the edge—but of course I didn't. Who does? Don't we all just keep doing the things that make us even more like ourselves?

As I lay in bed with a godawful headache, sunlight streamed through the open window, and so did the smell of good French coffee from the hotel kitchen downstairs.

Heinrich Eduard Jacob called coffee the "anti-Bacchus." By the middle of the seventeenth century, when it had filtered westward from the Middle East and begun to captivate Europe, its potential consumers were in dire need of sobering up. "The eyes, the blood-vessels, the senses of the men of those days were soused in beer," observed Jacob. "It choked their livers, their voices, and their hearts." The average Englishman drank three liters of beer a day—nearly two six-packs—and spent a lot of time bumping into lampposts and falling into gutters. Coffee was hailed as a salubrious alternative. As an anonymous poet put it in 1674, "When foggy Ale, leavying up mighty trains / Of muddy vapours, had besieg'd our Brains, / Then Heaven in Pity . . . / First sent amongst us this All-healing Berry."

Between 1645 and 1750, as coffeehouses sprang up in Paris, Vienna, Leipzig, Amsterdam, Rome, and Venice, the All-healing Berry defogged innumerable Continental brains. But until tea gained the upper hand around 1730, the English were the undisputed kings of coffee. By the most conservative estimates, London had five hundred coffeehouses at the turn of the eighteenth century. (If New York City were similarly equipped today, it would have nearly eight thousand.) These weren't merely places to drink the muddy liquid that one critic likened to "syrup of soot or essence of old shoes." In the days when public libraries were nonexistent and journalism was in its embryonic stages, they were a vital center of news, gossip, and education—"penny universities" whose main business, in the words of a 1657 newspaper ad, was "PUB-LICK INTERCOURSE."

London had a coffeehouse for everyone (as long as you were male). If you were a gambler, you went to White's. If you were a physician, you went to Garraway's or

Child's. If you were a businessman, you went to Lloyd's, which later evolved into the great insurance house. If you were a scientist, you went to the Grecian, where Isaac Newton, Edmund Halley, and Hans Sloane once staged a public dissection of a dolphin that had been caught in the Thames. If you were a journalist, you went to Button's, where Joseph Addison had set up a "Reader's Letter-box" shaped like a lion's head; you could post submissions to *The Guardian* in its mouth. And if you were a man of letters, you—along with Pope, Pepys, and Dryden—went to Will's, where you could join a debate on whether Milton should have written *Paradise Lost* in rhymed couplets instead of blank verse. These coffeehouses changed the course of English social history by demonstrating how pleasant it was to hang out in a place where (according to a 1674 set of Rules and Orders of the Coffee House) "Gentry, Tradesmen, all are welcome hither, / and may without affront sit down together." And they changed the course of English literature by turning monologuists into conversationalists. A 1705 watercolor that now hangs in the British Museum depicts a typical establishment, a high-ceilinged room dominated by a huge black coffee cauldron that simmers over a blazing fire. The periwigged patrons are sipping coffee, smoking pipes, reading news-sheets, and scribbling in notebooks, but most of all—you can tell from their gesticulations—they are talking.

Looking back, I see that my evenings in Dunster House were a penny university in miniature. It therefore saddens me to report that these days my coffee-drinking is usually a solitary affair, a Balzacian response to deadlines (though in smaller doses) rather than an opportunity for PUBLICK INTERCOURSE. Time is scarcer than it used to be; I make my coffee with a disposable paper filter stuffed into a little plastic cone, not in a *cafetière à piston*. My customary intake is only a cup or two a day—still with milk and sugar—though I ratchet up my consumption when I'm writing. In the spirit of participatory journalism, every word of this essay has been written under the influence of 1,3,7-trimethylxanthine, in quantities sufficient to justify the use, after a respite of thirty years, of the mug with the polka-dotted pig.

My coffee is in every way a weaker brew than it once was, but I could never give it up entirely. This is not just a matter of habit, sentiment, or taste; it is more akin to the reasons that, long ago, the Galla people of Ethiopia ate ground coffee mixed with animal fat before they went off to fight, or that the night before every battle of the Civil War, you would have seen hundreds of camp-fires flickering in the darkness, each surmounted by a pot of thick, black, courage-inducing coffee.

I remember a morning five years ago when I took a dawn flight to Fort Myers, Florida. My father had just been hospitalized with what looked like—and in fact turned out to be—terminal cancer, and the task of dealing with doctors, nurses, and hospice workers had fallen to me. I'd been up all night, and I stumbled off the plane so bleary I could hardly walk. There, shimmering like a mirage at the end of the jetway, in the midst of what on my last visit had been a wasteland of Pizza Huts and Burger Kings, stood a newly opened Starbucks.

I know, I know. Heartless corporate giant. Monster of coast-to-coast uniformity. Killer of mom-and-pop cafés. But that's not what I thought at that moment. I thought: I'm going to order a grande latte with whole milk. I'm going to pour in two packets of Sugar in the Raw, and stir really well so there are no undissolved crystals at the bottom. I'm going to sit down and drink it slowly. *Then* I'm going to drive to the hospital.

As I walked toward the counter, I said to myself: *I can do this.*

UNDER WATER

I was an impatient child who disliked obstructions: traffic jams, clogged bathtub drains, catsup bottles you had to bang. I liked to drop twigs into the stream that ran through our backyard and watch them float downstream, coaxed around rocks and branches by the distant pull of the ocean. If they hit a snag, I freed them.

When I was eighteen, rushing through life as fast as I could, I was a student on a month-long wilderness program in western Wyoming. On the third day of the course we went canoeing on the Green River, a tributary of the Colorado that begins in the glaciers of the Wind River range and flows south across the sagebrush plains. Swollen by warm-weather runoff from an unusually deep snowpack, the Green was higher and swifter that month—June of 1972—than it had been in forty years. A river at flood stage can have strange currents. There is not enough room in the channel for the water to move downstream in an orderly fashion, so it collides with itself and forms whirlpools and boils and souseholes. Our instructors decided to stick to their itinerary nevertheless, but they put in at a relatively easy section of the Green, one that the flood had merely upgraded, in the international system of whitewater classification, from Class I to Class II. There are six levels of difficulty, and Class II was not an unreasonable challenge for novice paddlers.

The Green River did not seem dangerous to me. It seemed magnificently unobstructed. Impediments to progress—the rocks and stranded trees that under normal conditions would protrude above the surface—were mostly submerged. The river carried our aluminum canoe high and lightly, like a child on a pair of broad shoulders. We could rest our paddles on the gunwales and let the water do our work. The sun was bright and hot. Every few minutes I dipped my bandanna in the river, draped it over my head, and let an ounce or two of melted glacier run down my neck.

I was in the bow of the third canoe. We rounded a bend and saw, fifty feet ahead, a standing wave in the wake of a large black boulder. The students in the lead canoe were attempting to avoid the boulder by backferrying, slipping crabwise across the current by angling their boat diagonally and stroking backward. Done right, backferrying allows paddlers to hover midstream and carefully plan their course instead of surrendering to the water's impetuous pace. But if they lean upstream—a natural inclination, as few people choose to lean toward the difficulties that lie ahead—the current can overflow the lowered gunwale and flip the boat. And that is what happened to the lead canoe.

I wasn't worried when I saw it go over. Knowing that we might capsize in the fast water, our instructors had arranged to have our gear trucked to our next campsite. The packs were safe. The water was little more than waist-deep, and the paddlers were both wearing life jackets. They would be fine. One was already scrambling onto the right-hand bank.

But where was the second paddler? Gary, a local boy from Rawlins a year or two younger than I, seemed to be hung up on something. He was standing at a strange angle in the middle of the river, just downstream from the boulder. Gary was the only student on the course who had not brought sneakers, and one of his mountaineering boots had become wedged between two rocks. The instructors would come around the bend in a moment and pluck him out, like a twig from a snag.

But they didn't come. The second canoe pulled over to the bank and ours followed. Thirty seconds passed, maybe a minute. Then we saw the standing wave bend Gary's body forward at the waist, push his face underwater, stretch his arms in front of him, and slip his orange life jacket off his shoulders. The life jacket lingered for a moment at his wrists before it floated downstream, its long white straps twisting in the current. His shirtless torso was pale and undulating, and it changed shape as hills and valleys of water flowed over him, altering the curve of the liquid lens through which we watched him. I thought: *He looks like the flayed skin of St. Bartholomew in the Sistine Chapel.* As soon as I had the thought, I knew that it was dishonorable. To think about anything outside the moment, outside Gary, was a crime of inattention. I swallowed a small, sour piece of self-knowledge: I was the sort of person who, instead of weeping or shouting or praying during a crisis, thought about something from a textbook (H. W. Janson's *History of Art*, page 360).

Once the flayed man had come, I could not stop the stream of images: Gary looked like a piece of seaweed, Gary looked like a waving handkerchief, Gary looked like a hula dancer. Each simile was a way to avoid thinking about what Gary *was*, a drowning boy. To remember these things is dishonorable, too, for I have long since forgotten Gary's last name and the color of his hair and the sound of his voice.

I do not remember a single word that anyone said. Somehow we got into one of the canoes, all five of us, and tried to ferry the twenty feet or so to the middle of the river. The current was so strong, and we were so incompetent, that we never even got close. Then we tried it on foot, linking arms to form a chain. The water was so cold that it stung. And it was noisy, not the roar and crash of whitewater but a groan, a terrible bass grumble, from the stones that were rolling and leaping down the riverbed. When we got close to Gary, we couldn't see him. All we could see was the reflection of the sky. A couple of times, groping blindly, one of us touched him, but he was as slippery as soap. Then our knees buckled and our elbows unlocked, and we rolled downstream, like the stones. The river's rocky load, moving invisibly beneath its smooth surface, pounded and scraped us. Eventually the current heaved us, blue-lipped and panting, onto the bank. In that other world above the water, the only sounds were the buzzing of bees and flies. Our wet sneakers kicked up red dust. The air smelled of sage and rabbitbrush and sunbaked earth.

We tried again and again, back and forth between the worlds. Wet, dry, cold, hot, turbulent, still.

At first I assumed that we would save him. He would lie on the bank and the sun would warm him while we administered mouth-to-mouth resuscitation. If we couldn't get him out, we would hold him upright in the river; maybe he could still breathe. But the Green River was flowing at nearly three thousand cubic feet—about ninety tons—per second. At that rate, water can wrap a canoe around a boulder like tinfoil. Water can uproot a tree. Water can squeeze the air out of a boy's lungs, undo knots, drag off a life jacket, lever a boot so tightly into the riverbed that even if we had had ropes—the ropes that were in the packs that were in the trucks—we never could have budged him.

We kept going in, not because we had any hope of saving Gary after the first ten minutes but because we needed to save face. It would have been humiliating if the instructors had come around the bend and found us sitting in the sagebrush, a docile row of five with no hypothermia and no skinned knees. Eventually, they did come. The boats had been delayed because one of them had nearly capsized, and the instructors had made the students stop and practice backferrying until they learned not to lean upstream. Even though Gary had already drowned, the instructors did all the same things we had done, more competently but no more effectively, because they, too, would have been humiliated if they hadn't skinned their knees. Men in wetsuits, belayed with ropes, pried the body out the next morning.

Twenty-seven years have passed. My life seems too fast now, so obstructions bother me less than they once did. I am no longer in a hurry to see what is around the next bend. I find myself wanting to backferry, to hover midstream, suspended. If I could do that, I might avoid many things: harsh words, foolish decisions, moments of inattention, regrets that wash over me, like water.

SOURCES

I am an enthusiastic amateur, not a scholar. My bookshelves and file cabinets resemble the nest of a magpie that collects shiny objects, with diamond rings tucked next to tinfoil candy wrappers. Though the bibliography that follows contains some valuable standard works and some obscure gems, along with some oddities, I'm sure it leaves out many helpful books that I would have known about, and made good use of, if I were an expert on any of the topics below.

PREFACE

The best recent works on the personal essay—and its subset, the familiar essay—are, unsurprisingly, by two of its leading practitioners, Joseph Epstein and Phillip Lopate. Those interested in the history of the essay may enjoy the online roundtable, a transcription of a radio conversation with four participants, including Epstein. Readers who share my enthusiasm for the work of Lamb and Hazlitt may be charmed, as I was, by the elegance with which Marie Hamilton Law captures the essential characteristics of the familiar essay.

Bryan, William Frank, and Ronald S. Crane. *The English Familiar Essay*. Boston: Atheneum Press, 1916.

Epstein, Joseph. "The Personal Essay: A Form of Discovery." In *The Norton Book of Personal Essays*, ed. Joseph Epstein. New York: W. W. Norton, 1997.

Epstein, Joseph, et al. "Roundtable: The History of the Essay." *Fourth Genre: Explorations in Nonfiction*, www.chsbs.cmich.edu/Robert_Root/background/Roundtable.html.

Fadiman, Clifton. "A Gentle Dirge for the Familiar Essay." In *Party of One*. Cleveland: World Publishing Company, 1955.

——. Introduction. In *Party of Twenty*. New York: Simon and Schuster, 1963.

Hazlitt, William. *Table-Talk: Essays on Men and Manners*. London: Grant Richards, 1903.

Law, Marie Hamilton. "The English Familiar Essay in the Early Nineteenth Century." Ph.D. diss. University of Pennsylvania, 1934. Reprint, New York: Russell and Russell, 1965.

Lopate, Phillip. Introduction. In *The Art of the Personal Essay: An Anthology from the Classical Era to the Present*. New York: Anchor Books, 1995.

Robertson, Stuart. *Familiar Essays*. New York: Prentice-Hall, 1930.

COLLECTING NATURE

Both my essay and my childhood owe a great deal to Alexander B. Klots's splendid field guide to butterflies. I am also particularly fond of—and drew many details from—David Elliston Allen's charming and learned book on amateur natural history in Britain.

Though the Darwin biography by Adrian Desmond and James Moore is admirable, those who know Darwin only from secondary sources should try the *Voyage of the* Beagle—and then move on to Darwin's captivating contemporaries, Alfred Russel Wallace and Henry Walter Bates.

Brian Boyd's two-volume biography of Nabokov is thoughtful and comprehensive. Readers of my essay already know that I consider the sixth chapter of Nabokov's *Speak, Memory* the holy grail of butterfly literature.

ON BUTTERFLIES

Antram, Charles B. *The Collecting and Preservation of Butterflies and Moths, with Practical Hints for Collecting in the Field*. Lymington, U.K.: Charles T. King, 1951.

Harman, Ian. *Collecting Butterflies and Moths*. London: Williams and Norgate, 1950.

Ingpen, Abel. *Instructions for Collecting, Rearing, and Preserving British & Foreign Insects.* London: William Smith, 1843.

Klots, Alexander B. *A Field Guide to the Butterflies of North America, East of the Great Plains.* Boston: Houghton Mifflin, 1951.

Packard, A. S., Jr. How to Collect and Observe Insects. Reprint from *The Maine Scientific Survey for 1862.* Augusta, Maine: Kennebec Journal, 1863.

On collecting in general

Elsner, John, and Roger Cardinal, eds. *The Cultures of Collecting.* Cambridge, Mass.: Harvard University Press, 1994.

Muensterberger, Werner. *Collecting: An Unruly Passion.* Princeton: Princeton University Press, 1994.

Pearce, Susan M. *On Collecting: An Investigation into Collecting in the European Tradition.* London: Routledge, 1995.

Theroux, Alexander. "Odd Collections." *The Yale Review* 86:1 (January 1998).

On natural history, especially nineteenth-century

Allen, David Elliston. *The Naturalist in Britain: A Social History.* Princeton: Princeton University Press, 1994.

Bates, Henry Walter. *The Naturalist on the River Amazons.* Intro. Alex Shoumatoff. New York: Penguin, 1989.

Kastner, Joseph. *A Species of Eternity.* New York: Alfred A. Knopf, 1977.

Ritvo, Harriet. *The Platypus and the Mermaid: And Other Figments of the Classifying Imagination.* Cambridge, Mass.: Harvard University Press, 1997.

Wallace, Alfred Russel. *Island Life: Or, the Phenomena and Causes of Insular Faunas and Floras.* London: Macmillan, 1902.

————. *The Malay Archipelago: The Land of the Orang-Utan and the Bird of Paradise, A Narrative of Travel, with Studies of Man and Nature.* London: Macmillan, 1886.

By and about Charles Darwin

Darwin, Charles. "Recollections of the Development of My Mind and Character." In Frederick William Roe, ed., *Victorian Prose.* New York: Ronald Press, 1947.

————. *Voyage of the* Beagle. London: Penguin, 1989.

Clark, Ronald W. *The Survival of Charles Darwin*. New York: Random House, 1984.

Desmond, Adrian, and James Moore. *Darwin*. London: Michael Joseph, 1991.

Huxley, Francis. "Charles Darwin: Life and Habit," parts 1 and 2. *The American Scholar* 28:4 (Autumn 1959) and 29:1 (Winter 1959/60).

Marks, Richard Lee. *Three Men of the* Beagle. New York: Alfred A. Knopf, 1991.

BY AND ABOUT VLADIMIR NABOKOV

Appel, Alfred, Jr. Notes to *The Annotated Lolita: Revised and Updated*. New York: Vintage, 1991.

Boyd, Brian. *Vladimir Nabokov: The American Years*. Princeton: Princeton University Press, 1991.

————. *Vladimir Nabokov: The Russian Years*. Princeton: Princeton University Press, 1990.

Boyd, Brian, and Kurt Johnson. "Nabokov, Scientist." *Natural History*, July–August 1999.

Coates, Steve. "Nabokov's Work, on Butterflies, Stands the Test of Time." *New York Times*, May 27, 1997.

Field, Andrew. *Nabokov: His Life in Art*. Boston: Little, Brown, 1967.

Johnson, Kurt, and Steve Coates. *Nabokov's Blues: The Scientific Odyssey of a Literary Genius*. Cambridge, Mass.: Zoland, 1999.

Johnson, Kurt, G. Warren Whitaker, and Zsolt Bálint. "Nabokov as Lepidopterist: An Informed Appraisal." *Nabokov Studies* 3 (1996).

Nabokov, Vladimir. "The Aurelian." In *Nabokov's Dozen: A Collection of Thirteen Stories*. New York: Avon, 1973.

————. "Christmas." In *Details of a Sunset and Other Stories*. New York: McGraw-Hill, 1976.

————. *Pale Fire*. New York: G. P. Putnam's Sons, 1962.

————. *Speak, Memory*. New York: Pyramid, 1968.

Pick, Nancy. "Vladimir Nabokov's Genitalia Cabinet." In *The Rarest of the Rare*. New York: HarperCollins, 2004.

Miscellaneous sources

Dickens, Charles. *Our Mutual Friend*. London: Penguin, 1985.

Fowles, John. *The Collector*. Boston: Little, Brown, 1997.

Jones, James H. *Alfred C. Kinsey: A Public/Private Life*. New York: W. W.
Norton, 1997.

The Unfuzzy Lamb

Winifred F. Courtney's biography of the young Lamb was especially useful. For contemporary perspectives, see the Hazlitt essay and the brief
memoir by Thomas Noon Talfourd at the end of Lamb's *Literary
Sketches and Letters*, both of which vividly capture the weekly soirées
Charles and Mary Lamb held in their lodgings at No. 4 Inner Temple
Lane. Chapter 16 of Leigh Hunt's autobiography also contains a graceful
tribute to Lamb.

By Charles Lamb

Lamb, Charles. *Charles Lamb & the Lloyds: Comprising Newly-Discovered
Letters of Charles Lamb, Samuel Taylor Coleridge, The Lloyds, Etc.*,
ed. E. V. Lucas. Philadelphia: J. B. Lippincott, 1899.

————. *The Complete Works in Prose and Verse of Charles Lamb*, ed.
R. H. Shepherd. Boston: De Wolfe, Fiske, and Company. Undated.

————. *The Essays of Elia*. London: Edward Moxon and Company,
1867.

————. *Everybody's Lamb: Being a Selection from the Essays of Elia, the
Letters and the Miscellaneous Prose of Charles Lamb*, ed. A. C. Ward.
London: G. Bell and Sons, 1933.

————. *Literary Sketches and Letters: Being the Final Memorials of
Charles Lamb*, ed. Thomas Noon Talfourd. New York: D. Appleton
and Company, 1849.

————. *The Life and Works of Charles Lamb*. Vol. 1, *The Letters of
Charles Lamb*, ed. Alfred Ainger. New York: International Publishing Company. Undated.

————. *The Life and Works of Charles Lamb*. Vol. 2, *Poems, Plays and*

Miscellaneous Essays, ed. Alfred Ainger. New York: International Publishing Company. Undated.

———. *The Works of Charles Lamb in Five Volumes*. New York: A. C. Armstrong and Son, 1885.

ON CHARLES LAMB

Barnett, George L. *Charles Lamb*. Boston: Twayne Publishers, 1976.

Burton, Sarah. *A Double Life: A Biography of Charles and Mary Lamb*. London: Penguin, 2004.

Courtney, Winifred F. *Young Charles Lamb, 1775–1802*. New York: New York University Press, 1982.

Cruse, Amy. "A Supper at Charles Lamb's." In *Bouillabaisse for Bibliophiles*, ed. William Targ. Cleveland: World Publishing Company, 1955.

Frank, Robert. *Don't Call Me Gentle Charles!* Corvallis: Oregon State University Press, 1976.

Hazlitt, William. "On the Conversation of Authors." In *The Essays of William Hazlitt*, ed. Catherine MacDonald MacLean. New York: Coward-McCann, 1950.

Hunt, Leigh. *The Autobiography of Leigh Hunt*, ed. J. E. Morpurgo. London: Cresset, 1949.

Johnson, Edith Christina. "Lamb and Coleridge." *The American Scholar* 6:2 (Spring 1937).

Prance, Claude A. *Companion to Charles Lamb: A Guide to People and Places, 1760–1847*. London: Mansell, 1983.

ICE CREAM

I could not have written the section on the history of ice cream without Elizabeth David's exemplary book.

A note for the pedantic: Several sources—including myself, in an earlier version of this essay—have erroneously cited 1700, not 1744, as the year of the first recorded ice-cream consumption in America. Thomas Bladen, one of Maryland's colonial governors, served it to a group of Virginia commissioners on their way to a meeting with the Iroquois nation. Bladen was born in 1698 and is unlikely to have been a dinner host at age two.

Burke, A. D. *Practical Ice Cream Making*. Milwaukee: Olsen, 1947.

David, Elizabeth. *Harvest of the Cold Months: The Social History of Ice and Ices*. London: Michael Joseph, 1994.

Dickson, Paul. *The Great American Ice Cream Book*. New York: Atheneum, 1973.

"Flying Fortresses Double as Ice-Cream Freezers." *New York Times*, March 13, 1943.

Geeslin, Campbell, ed. *The Nobel Prize Annual 1991*. New York: International Management Group, 1992.

Gilbert, Susan. "Headaches Come in Icy Flavors." *New York Times*, May 14, 1997.

Grimes, William. "In the Ice Cream Follies, Anything Goes." *New York Times*, August 5, 1998.

Herszenhorn, David M. "A Town's Last Word to the Ice Cream Man: Quiet!" *New York Times*, March 4, 1998.

Keeney, Philip G. "Ice Cream Manufacture." *Course 102, Correspondence Courses in Agriculture, Family Living and Community Development*. University Park, Pa.: Pennsylvania State University.

McGee, Harold. *On Food and Cooking: The Science and Lore of the Kitchen*. New York: Charles Scribner's Sons, 1984.

Nieves, Evelyn. "Savoring Legal Success, an Ice Cream Vendor Calls the Tune." *New York Times*, May 7, 1998.

Skow, John. "They All Scream for It." *Time*, August 10, 1981.

NIGHT OWL

Among the literary sources, my favorite is the Dickens essay. For atmosphere and eclecticism, the indispensable night author is A. Alvarez, who writes about everything from hypnagogic hallucinations to an all-night "ride-along" in a New York City patrol car. Although his book does not concentrate primarily on literary topics, he writes so beautifully that I believe *Night* itself is likely to be remembered as a work of literature.

LITERARY SOURCES

Alvarez, A. *Night*. New York: W. W. Norton, 1995.

Carroll, Lewis. "Pillow Problems." In *Night Walks: A Bedside Companion*, ed. Joyce Carol Oates. Princeton: Ontario Review Press, 1982.

Dickens, Charles. "Night Walks." In *The Uncommercial Traveller*. New York: Macmillan, 1896.

Dreifus, Claudia. "A Conversation with John McPhee." *New York Times*, November 17, 1998.

Fadiman, Clifton. "It's a Puzzlement." In *Worth a Jot* (unpublished manuscript).

Fitzgerald, F. Scott. "Sleeping and Waking." In *The Literary Insomniac*, ed. Elyse Cheney and Wendy Hubbert. New York: Doubleday, 1996.

Jackson, Holbrook. "Specimen Days." In *Bookman's Pleasure*. New York: Farrar, Straus and Company, 1947.

Lamb, Charles. "Popular Fallacies: That We Should Lie Down with the Lamb." In *The Essays of Elia*. London: Edward Moxon and Company, 1867.

Proulx, E. Annie. "Waking Up." In *The Literary Insomniac*, ed. Elyse Cheney and Wendy Hubbert. New York: Doubleday, 1996.

Spender, Stephen. Interview. In *Writers at Work: The Paris Review Interviews, Sixth Series*, ed. George Plimpton. New York: Viking, 1984.

Thomson, James. "The City of Dreadful Night." In *Poetry of the Victorian Period*, ed. Jerome Hamilton Buckley and George Benjamin Woods. Glenview, Ill.: Scott, Foresman and Company, 1965.

Whitman, Walt. "Song of Myself." In *Whitman*, ed. Robert Creeley. Harmondsworth, U.K.: Penguin, 1973.

Young, Edward. *Night Thoughts, or, the Complaint and the Consolation*. Mineola, N.Y.: Dover, 1975.

MISCELLANEOUS SOURCES

Blakeslee, Sandra. "Biologists Close In on the 'Tick-Tock' Genes." *New York Times*, December 15, 1998.

Goode, Erica. "New Hope for the Losers in the Battle to Stay Awake." *New York Times*, November 3, 1998.

Lamberg, Lynne. *Bodyrhythms: Chronobiology and Peak Performance.*
    New York: William Morrow, 1994.

Melbin, Murray. *Night as Frontier: Colonizing the World After Dark.* New
    York: Free Press, 1987.

Miller, Louise. *Careers for Night Owls & Other Insomniacs.* Chicago:
    VGM Career Horizons, 1995.

Moore-Ede, Martin C., Frank M. Sulzman, and Charles A. Fuller. *The
    Clocks That Time Us: Physiology of the Circadian Timing System.*
    Cambridge, Mass.: Harvard University Press, 1982.

PROCRUSTES AND
THE CULTURE WARS

This essay is loosely adapted from talks given to the Phi Beta Kappa chap-
ters of Yale College, Harvard College, the University of Nebraska at Lin-
coln, and Gettysburg College. Part of it focuses on Ralph Waldo Emerson
because the year I delivered the Harvard Phi Beta Kappa Oration happened to be the 160th anniversary of Emerson's 1837 Harvard Phi Beta
Kappa Oration, "The American Scholar."

ON THE CULTURE WARS AND THE LITERARY CANON

Anson, J. Cameron. Letter. *Harper's Magazine*, April 1996.

Arendt, Hannah. "The Crisis in Culture: Its Social and Its Political Sig-
    nificance." In *Between Past and Future*. New York: Penguin, 1993.

Arnold, Matthew. "Wordsworth." In *Criticism: The Major Texts*, ed. Wal-
    ter Jackson Bate. New York: Harcourt, Brace and World, 1952.

Denby, David. *Great Books: My Adventures with Homer, Rousseau, Woolf,
    and Other Indestructible Writers of the Western World.* New York: Si-
    mon and Schuster, 1996.

Kaplan, Justin. "Selling 'Huck Finn' Down the River." *New York Times
    Book Review*, March 10, 1996.

Ronholt, Sharon Uemura. Letter. *New York Times Book Review*, January
    19, 1997.

Smiley, Jane. "Say It Ain't So, Huck." *Harper's Magazine*, January 1996.

Twain, Mark. *The Adventures of Huckleberry Finn.* New York: Modern
    Library, 2001.

Weiss, Philip. "Herman-Neutics." *New York Times Magazine*, December 15, 1996.

On Procrustes and Theseus

Apollodorus, *The Library*, vol. 2, trans. James George Frazer. Cambridge, Mass.: Loeb Classical Library, 1970.

Diodorus Siculus. *Bibliotheca Historica*. Stuttgart: Teubner, 1985–1991. Unpublished translation of Book 4, 59.2 by Adam Goodheart.

Graves, Robert. *The Greek Myths: Complete Edition*. London: Penguin, 1992.

Hamilton, Edith. *Mythology*. New York: Mentor, 1962.

Hyginus. *The Myths of Hyginus*, trans. Mary Grant. Lawrence: University of Kansas Press, 1960.

Larousse Encyclopedia of Mythology. New York: Prometheus, 1959.

Ovid, *The Metamorphoses of Ovid*, trans. Allen Mandelbaum. New York: Harcourt Brace, 1993.

Plutarch. *Lives: Theseus and Romulus, Lycurgus and Numa, Solon and Publicola*, trans. Bernadotte Perrin. Cambridge, Mass.: Loeb Classical Library, 1993.

On James Stockdale and Epictetus

Admiral Stockdale: The Official Site for Admiral James B. Stockdale, www.admiralstockdale.us.

Epictetus. *The Enchiridion*, trans. Elizabeth Carter. *The Internet Classics Archive*, classics.mit.edu/Epictetus/epicench.html.

Stockdale, James B. *Courage Under Fire: Testing Epictetus's Doctrines in a Laboratory of Human Behavior*. Stanford: Hoover Institution Press, 1993.

———. *Thoughts of a Philosophical Fighter Pilot*. Stanford: Hoover Institution Press, 1995.

———. *A Vietnam Experience: Ten Years of Reflection*. Stanford: Hoover Institution Press, 1984.

On Ralph Waldo Emerson

Chapman, John Jay. "Emerson, Sixty Years After." *The Atlantic Monthly*, January 1897.

Emerson, Ralph Waldo. "The American Scholar." In *Selected Essays*. New York: Penguin, 1985.

McAleer, John. *Ralph Waldo Emerson: Days of Encounter*. Boston: Little, Brown, 1984.

Richardson, Robert D., Jr. *Emerson: The Mind on Fire*. Berkeley: University of California Press, 1995.

ON THE QUARREL OF THE ANCIENTS AND THE MODERNS

Nelson, Robert J. "The Quarrel of the Ancients and the Moderns." In *A New History of French Literature*, ed. Denis Hollier. Cambridge, Mass.: Harvard University Press, 1989.

Swift, Jonathan. "The Battle of the Books." In *A Tale of a Tub and Other Works*. Oxford: Oxford University Press, 1990.

COLERIDGE THE RUNAWAY

This essay describes my journey through Richard Holmes's biography of Coleridge, and most of it is therefore drawn from those two magical volumes. I also admire Walter Jackson Bate's brief but perceptive biography. Leigh Hunt's autobiography, also mentioned in the sources for the Charles Lamb essay, includes a memorable portrait of Coleridge. The online Samuel Taylor Coleridge Archive contains many useful links.

Bate, Walter Jackson. *Coleridge*. New York: Macmillan, 1968.

Coleridge, Samuel Taylor. *Biographia Literaria*. Princeton: Princeton University Press, 1985.

———. *Collected Letters of Samuel Taylor Coleridge*, vol. 5: 1820–1825, ed. Earl Leslie Griggs. Oxford: Oxford University Press, 1971.

———. *Selected Poetry and Prose of Coleridge*, ed. Donald A. Stauffer. New York: Modern Library, 1951.

Forster, E. M. "Trooper Silas Tomkyn Comberbacke." In *Abinger Harvest*. New York: Harcourt and Brace, 1964.

Holmes, Richard. *Coleridge: Darker Reflections, 1804–1834*. New York: Pantheon, 1999.

———. *Coleridge: Early Visions, 1772–1804*. New York: Viking, 1990.

Hunt, Leigh. *The Autobiography of Leigh Hunt*, ed. J. E. Morpurgo. London: Cresset, 1949.

Johnson, Edith Christina. "Lamb and Coleridge." *The American Scholar* 6:2 (Spring 1937).

Perkins, David, ed. *English Romantic Writers*. New York: Harcourt, Brace and World, 1967.

Saintsbury, George. "Lesser Poets, 1790–1837: Hartley Coleridge." *Cambridge History of English and American Literature*, vol. 12. New York: G. P. Putnam's Sons, 1907–1921.

Tiefert, Marjorie A. *The Samuel Taylor Coleridge Archive*, etext .virginia.edu/stc/Coleridge/stc.html.

Wordsworth, William, and Samuel Taylor Coleridge. *Lyrical Ballads*. London: Penguin, 1999.

MAIL

I relied extensively on Christopher Browne's lively history of British mail and Bernhard Siegert's imaginative study of the connections between the postal system and literature.

The last name of Jean-Jacques Renouard de Villayer, the man who invented the paper wrapper that some historians view as a proto-stamp, is sometimes spelled "Vélayer." I opted for "Villayer" because it's the spelling used by most philatelic scholars as well as on a 1944 French commemorative stamp.

ON POSTAL AND EPISTOLARY HISTORY

Barker, G. E. "The 'Billets de Port Payé' of 1653." *Journal of the France and Colonies Philatelic Society* 35:2 (June 1985).

Browne, Christopher. *Getting the Message: The Story of the British Post Office*. Phoenix Mill, U.K.: Alan Sutton, 1993.

Bruns, James H. *Mail on the Move*. Polo, Ill.: Transportation Trails, 1992.

Carroll, Andrew, ed. *Letters of a Nation*. New York: Broadway, 1999.

Pryor, Felix, ed. *The Faber Book of Letters: Letters Written in the English Language, 1578–1939*. London: Faber and Faber, 1988.

Siegert, Bernhard. *Relays: Literature as an Epoch of the Postal System*, trans. Kevin Repp. Stanford: Stanford University Press, 1999.

Wood, Kenneth A. *Post Dates: A Chronology of Intriguing Events in the Mails and Philately*. Albany, Oreg.: Van Dahl, 1985.

ON E-MAIL

Ardell, Donald B. *The Smileys and Acronyms Dictionary*, www.seek wellness.com/wellness/smiley_file.htm.

Flynn, Nancy, and Tom Flynn. *Writing Effective E-Mail*. Menlo Park: Crisp, 1998.

Gil, Paul. *Glossary of Internet Abbreviations: Email and Chat Shorthand!* netforbeginners.about.com/cs/netiquette101/a/abbreviations.htm.

Gopnik, Adam. "The Return of the Word." *The New Yorker*, December 6, 1999.

"Netiquette 101 for New Netizens," www.microsoft.com/southafrica/ athome/security/online/netiquette.mspx.

The Unofficial Smiley Dictionary. In *EFF's (Extended) Guide to the Internet*, www.eff.org/Net_culture/Net_info/EFF_Net_Guide/EEGTTI _HTML/eeg_286.html.

MISCELLANEOUS SOURCES

Barnett, George L. *Charles Lamb*. Boston: Twayne Publishers, 1976.

Crane, Hart. "My Grandmother's Love Letters." In *The Complete Poems and Selected Letters and Prose*. Garden City, N.Y.: Anchor, 1966.

Fadiman, Clifton. "Life's Minor Pleasures." In *Any Number Can Play*. Cleveland: World Publishing Company, 1957.

Houghton, Walter E. *The Victorian Frame of Mind, 1830–1870*. New Haven: Yale University Press, 1971.

Richardson, Samuel. *Clarissa; or, the History of a Young Lady*. London: Penguin Classics, 1986.

Sutherland, James, ed. *The Oxford Book of Literary Anecdotes*. New York: Touchstone, 1977.

Zaslaw, Neal, and William Cowdery, eds. *The Compleat Mozart: A Guide to the Musical Works of Wolfgang Amadeus Mozart*. New York: W. W. Norton, 1990.

MOVING

Persuasion is the wittiest novel about moving I know, but *A Little Princess* remains the most poignant—as tear-inducing today as it was when I first read it at age seven—because of the unexpected changes it rings on the theme of attempting to make a home for oneself in an alien place.

Though family lore and some scholars hold that James Montgomery Whitmore was killed by Paiute Indians (an account supported by the fact that five Paiutes were captured with money and articles that had belonged to Whitmore and his companion), several sources suggest that Navajos may have been responsible.

ON MOVING

Brown, Patricia Leigh. "For Sale: Everything but the Props." *New York Times,* February 10, 2000.

Jasper, James M. *Restless Nation: Starting Over in America.* Chicago: University of Chicago Press, 2000.

"Setting the Stage." *Rock Talk: The Magazine for Prudential Real Estate Professionals,* Spring 1998.

ON MY GREAT-GREAT-GRANDFATHERS
JAMES MONTGOMERY WHITMORE AND JOHN SHARP

Carter, Kate B., ed. *Our Pioneer Heritage,* vols. 1 and 9. Salt Lake City: Daughters of Utah Pioneers, 1958.

Esshom, Frank. *Pioneers and Prominent Men of Utah.* Salt Lake City: Utah Pioneers, 1913.

Jenson, Andrew. *Latter-Day Saint Biographical Encyclopedia,* vol. 1. Salt Lake City: Andrew Jenson History, 1901.

Lavender, David. *The History of Arizona's Pipe Spring National Monument.* Salt Lake City: Paragon, 1997.

Martin, Ruth J., ed. *Twentieth Ward History, 1856–1979.* Salt Lake City: Twentieth Ward History Committee, 1979.

"Public Workers: John Sharp." *The Improvement Era,* February 1904.

Raynor, W. A. *The Everlasting Spires: A Story of the Salt Lake Temple.* Salt Lake City: Deseret, 1965.

Warrum, Noble, ed. *Utah Since Statehood: Historical and Biographical*, vol. 4. Chicago: S. J. Clarke, 1919.

NOVELS

Austen, Jane. *Persuasion*. New York: Bantam, 1989.

Burnett, Frances Hodgson. *A Little Princess*. New York: Charles Scribner's Sons, 1932.

———. *The Secret Garden*. Philadelphia: Lippincott, 1962.

Dickens, Charles. *Martin Chuzzlewit*. London: Penguin, 1986.

Lewis, Sinclair. *Main Street*. New York: Signet Classics, 1998.

Steinbeck, John. *The Grapes of Wrath*. New York: Penguin, 1976.

Wilder, Laura Ingalls. The *Little House* series. New York: HarperTrophy, 1971.

A PIECE OF COTTON

The most helpful historical sources were Robert Justin Goldstein's richly annotated collection of primary documents on flag desecration and Scot M. Guenter's thought-provoking study of how the flag's meaning has changed over time.

ON THE HISTORY OF THE AMERICAN FLAG

Goldstein, Robert Justin, ed. *Desecrating the American Flag: Key Documents of the Controversy from the Civil War to 1995*. Syracuse: Syracuse University Press, 1996.

Guenter, Scot M. *The American Flag, 1777–1924: Cultural Shifts from Creation to Codification*. Rutherford, N.J.: Fairleigh Dickinson University Press, 1990.

Hinrichs, Kit, and Delphine Hirasuna. *Long May She Wave: A Graphic History of the American Flag*. Berkeley: Ten Speed Press, 2001.

Keenan, Marney Rich. "Stars & Stripes: Chicago Exhibit Attracts Unflagging Criticism." *Detroit News*, March 19, 1989.

Loeffelbein, Robert L. *The United States Flagbook: Everything about Old Glory*. Jefferson, N.C.: McFarland & Company, 1996.

Sedeen, Margaret. *Star-Spangled Banner: Our Nation and Its Flag*. Washington, D.C.: National Geographic Society, 1993.

West, Delno C., and Jean M. West. *Uncle Sam and Old Glory: Symbols of America*. New York: Atheneum, 2000.

ON THE FLAG AFTER 9/11

Dewan, Shaila K. "The Tattooed Badge of Courage." *New York Times*, September 30, 2001.

Grimes, William. "On Menus Everywhere, a Big Slice of Patriotism." *New York Times*, October 24, 2001.

Haberman, Clyde. "60's Lessons on How Not to Wave Flag." *New York Times*, September 19, 2001.

Marling, Karal Ann. "The Stars and Stripes, American Chameleon." *Chronicle of Higher Education*, October 26, 2001.

Packer, George. "Recapturing the Flag." *New York Times Magazine*, September 30, 2001.

Pollitt, Katha. "Put Out No Flags." *The Nation*, October 8, 2001.

"Torn U.S. Flag from Trade Center Rubble Has New Life." Reuters, November 1, 2001.

Welch, Liz. "Stamp Act." *New York Times Magazine*, October 21, 2001.

THE ARCTIC HEDONIST

The biographies of Stefansson by Richard Diubaldo and William R. Hunt are the most complete and least biased. D. M. LeBourdais, a longtime Stefansson colleague, and Erick Berry, a writer for young adults, place Stefansson on a pedestal; Jennifer Niven knocks him off. Despite its one-sidedness, Niven's book, from which I drew many particulars, provides the most detailed account of the *Karluk* disaster. The understandably angry memoir by McKinlay, a *Karluk* survivor, is also worth reading. In *The Friendly Arctic*, Stefansson gives his own fascinating, if self-serving, account of the ill-starred Canadian Arctic Expedition of 1913–1918 (his third arctic foray), of which the *Karluk* expedition was only one branch. In addition to the eleven *Karluk* men who died, five men in the expedition's southern party were lost, two of them while attempting to rescue Stefansson, who had failed to return to Banks Island on schedule. (In fact, he was happily mapping and exploring the area and was in no need of rescue.)

BY VILHJALMUR STEFANSSON

Stefansson, Vilhjalmur. *Arctic Manual.* New York: Macmillan, 1944.

———. *Discovery: The Autobiography of Vilhjalmur Stefansson.* New York: McGraw-Hill, 1964.

———. *The Friendly Arctic.* New York: Macmillan, 1922.

———. *My Life with the Eskimo.* New York: Collier, 1962.

———. *The Northward Course of Empire.* New York: Macmillan, 1924.

———. *Unsolved Mysteries of the Arctic.* New York: Macmillan, 1938.

———. *Writing on Ice: The Ethnographic Notebooks of Vilhjalmur Stefansson,* ed. Gísli Pálsson. Hanover, N.H.: University Press of New England, 2001.

———, ed. *Great Adventures and Explorations.* New York: Dial, 1947.

ON VILHJALMUR STEFANSSON

Berry, Erick. *Mr. Arctic.* New York: David McKay, 1966.

Diubaldo, Richard. *Stefansson and the Canadian Arctic.* Montreal: McGill-Queen's University Press, 1978.

Hunt, William R. *Stef: A Biography of Vilhjalmur Stefansson.* Vancouver: University of British Columbia Press, 1986.

LeBourdais, D. M. *Stefansson, Ambassador of the North.* Montreal: Harvest House, 1963.

McKinlay, William Laird. *The Last Voyage of the* Karluk. New York: St. Martin's Griffin, 1976.

Niven, Jennifer. *The Ice Master: The Doomed 1913 Voyage of the* Karluk. New York: Hyperion, 2000.

ON THE HISTORY OF ARCTIC EXPLORATION

Berton, Pierre. *The Arctic Grail: The Quest for the North West Passage and the North Pole, 1818–1909.* New York: Penguin, 1989.

Holland, Clive, ed. *Farthest North.* New York: Carroll and Graf, 1999.

Imbert, Bertrand. *North Pole, South Pole.* New York: Harry N. Abrams, 1992.

Mirsky, Jeannette. *To the Arctic! The Story of Northern Exploration from Earliest Times to the Present.* Intro. Vilhjalmur Stefansson. New York: Alfred A. Knopf, 1948.

Miscellaneous Sources

Fadiman, Clifton. "I Shook Hands with Shakespeare." In *Any Number Can Play*. Cleveland: World Publishing Company, 1957.

Hahn, J. G. von. "How the Dragon Was Tricked." In *The Pink Fairy Book*, ed. Andrew Lang. New York: Dover, 1967.

Wolfe, Tom. *The Right Stuff*. New York: Farrar, Straus and Giroux, 1979.

Coffee

The classic history is by Heinrich Eduard Jacob, who also happens to be an enormously enjoyable literary stylist. I drew much excellent material from Mark Pendergrast, Wolfgang Schivelbusch, and Bennett Alan Weinberg and Bonnie K. Bealer (to whom I owe the London–New York coffeehouse extrapolation). By far the most entertaining author on my coffee shelf is Stewart Lee Allen; he is best appreciated in a highly caffeinated state.

Much good writing has been done on (and in) coffeehouses. My favorite sources are Thomas Babington Macaulay's famous passage on coffeehouses as a political institution in late-seventeenth-century London and Harold V. Routh's seminal studies on the influence of coffeehouse conversation on English literature.

In case any readers have wondered how I could possibly remember what I ate for lunch more than three decades ago, my source for the menu of La Pyramide, Fernand Point's legendary restaurant in Vienne, is a breathless six-page aerogramme I sent my parents on July 21, 1969. I found it in their files after their deaths.

On Coffee in General

Allen, Stewart Lee. *The Devil's Cup: Coffee, the Driving Force in History*. New York: Soho, 1999.

Barefoot, Kevin, ed. *Higher Grounds: The Little Book of Coffee Culture*. Vancouver: Arsenal Pulp, 1995.

Dicum, Gregory, and Nina Luttinger. *The Coffee Book: Anatomy of an Industry from Crop to the Last Drop*. New York: New Press, 1999.

Jacob, Heinrich Eduard. *The Epic of a Commodity*, trans. Eden and Cedar Paul [1935]. Intro. Lynn Alley. Short Hills, N.J.: Burford, 1998.

Pendergrast, Mark. *Uncommon Grounds: The History of Coffee and How It Transformed Our World.* New York: Basic, 1999.

Schivelbusch, Wolfgang. *Tastes of Paradise: A Social History of Spices, Stimulants, and Intoxicants*, trans. David Jacobson. New York: Pantheon, 1992.

Weinberg, Bennett Alan, and Bonnie K. Bealer. *The World of Caffeine: The Science and Culture of the World's Most Popular Drug.* New York: Routledge, 2002.

Yates, Jill. *Coffee Lover's Bible.* Santa Fe: Clear Light, 1998.

ON THE HISTORY OF COFFEEHOUSES

"The Character of a Coffee-House" (1673) and "Coffee-Houses Vindicated" (1675). In Charles W. Colby, ed. *Selections from the Sources of English History, B.C. 55–A.D. 1832.* London: Longmans, Green, 1920.

Ellis, Markman. "An Introduction to the Coffee-House: A Discursive Model." In Kahve-Society, *A Coffee-House Conversation on the International Art World and Its Exclusions.* E-book published in 2002 by Kahve-Society in collaboration with Autograph and the Institute of Digital Art Technology, www.kahve-house.com/society/programme.

Heise, Ulla. *Coffee and Coffee-Houses*, trans. Paul Roper. West Chester, Pa.: Schiffer, 1987.

Macaulay, Thomas Babington. "The State of England in 1685: The Coffee Houses." In *The History of England from the Accession of James II*, vol. 1. New York: Harper and Brothers, 1856.

Pelzer, John, and Linda Pelzer. "The Coffee Houses of Augustan London." *History Today*, October 1982.

Pepys, Samuel. *The Diary of Samuel Pepys.* New York: Modern Library, 2001.

Routh, Harold V. "The Advent of Modern Thought in Popular Literature: Coffee-houses." In *Cambridge History of English and American Literature*, vol. 7. New York: G. P. Putnam's Sons, 1907–1921.

————. "Steele and Addison," "Influence of the Coffeehouses," "Literature and Clubland," and "Beginnings of *The Tatler*." In *Cambridge History of English and American Literature*, vol. 9. New York: G. P. Putnam's Sons, 1907–1921.

ON HONORÉ DE BALZAC AND COFFEE

Balzac, Honoré de. *Traité des excitants moderne*, trans. Robert Onopa. In Weinberg and Bealer, *The World of Caffeine*.

Pritchett, V. S. "Honoré de Balzac: Poor Relations." In *The Pritchett Century*. New York: Modern Library, 1999.

MISCELLANEOUS SOURCES

Jeffries, Stuart. "Secrets and Pies." *The Guardian*, March 19, 2003.

Plant, Sadie. *Writing on Drugs*. New York: Picador, 2001.

UNDER WATER

The Wyoming Water Resources Data System provided the information on the Green River's flood conditions in June of 1972.

After I read this essay at Wesleyan University in 2005, a man in the audience—Bill Johnston, a professor of Asian history—introduced himself. He told me that the boy who had drowned in the Green River had been his best friend when they were teenagers in Rawlins, Wyoming. I had written that I had forgotten Gary's last name, the color of his hair, and the sound of his voice. Now I know that Gary's last name was Hall, and his hair was blond.

ACKNOWLEDGMENTS

Eleven of these essays first appeared in *The American Scholar*. I've made minor changes in all of them. (For the compulsive writer, few things are more satisfying than reinstating a sentence that didn't fit the allotted space or de-clunking a phrase whose off-rhythm has been jangling in your head for years.) My seven years at the *Scholar* were bliss. I have never had, and probably will never have again, such kind and careful colleagues as Jean Stipicevic and Sandra Costich. They worked on these essays after midnight, before dawn, and on Christmas Eve, adjudicating fine points of grammar and, through their combination of intelligence and good humor, serving both as dear comrades-in-arms and as ideal readers. John Bethell, my mentor since college, is a consummate wordsmith whose 2:00 A.M. e-mails were familiar essays in miniature. He edited my paragraphs with attention and artistry and confirmed that there is no greater pleasure than working alongside a friend. Bill Whitworth gave me daily instruction in the English language. Aaron Matz energetically ferreted out sources and plugged fact-holes.

Several friends lent warm hands. Adam Goodheart dispensed sterling editorial counsel, told me about French coffeepots and Sicilian *granite*, and, on a desperate afternoon when I couldn't find an English version of Diodorus Siculus's description of Procrustes, translated the Greek. Alex Soojung-Kim Pang guided my reading of Darwin and Wallace during a fellowship year at Stanford and suggested sources on natural history, e-mail, and English coffeehouses. Peter Gradjansky refreshed my memory of our coffee-drinking rituals in Dunster F-13. Charlie Monheim recalled the night we saw Halley's Comet from the Tasman Glacier. My aunt Carol Whitmore filled me in on my pioneer great-great-grandfathers. Hugh Bethell, Dan Fromson, Campbell Geeslin, Nancy Pick, Henry Singer, and Evelyn Toynton gave me help of various kinds. My friendships with Jane Condon, Maud Gleason, Lou Ann Walker, and Tina Rathborne were wellsprings, as they have been for more than thirty years.

How many writers can say that their publishing house is also a home? I've felt that way about Farrar, Straus and Giroux since the day fourteen years ago when my remarkable editor, Jonathan Galassi, called to tell me he was going to publish my first book. I would also like to thank Corinna Barsan, Susan Goldfarb, Jim Guida, Jonathan Lippincott, Susan Mitchell, and Zachary Woolfe.

I am indebted to Dorothy Wickenden at *The New Yorker* for asking me to write "Under Water" and to Deborah Treisman for editing it so sensitively.

No literary agent could do more for a writer than Robert Lescher has done for me.

The following scholars and librarians generously shared their expertise as well as the resources of their institutions: Philip Cronenwett, formerly Special Collections Librarian at the Dartmouth College Library and now director of the Burndy Library; Doug Hesse, the Marsico Writing Program at the University of Denver; Frans Jorissen, the Académie Française de Philatélie; Carl H. Klaus, the Nonfiction Writing Program at the University of Iowa; Heather Lane, the Scott Polar Research Institute at Cambridge University; Ken Lawrence, the American Philatelic Society; Andre Mignault, the Museum of Comparative Zoology at Harvard; James Mitchell, New York University Library; Ellen Peachey, the American Philatelic Research Library; Nick Roberts, the Punch Cartoon Library in London; and Bonnie Turner, Sterling Memorial Library at Yale.

I am grateful to my children, Susannah and Henry, for indulging my weakness for shells and butterflies and, whenever they saw twenty books open on my desk and twenty more on the floor, realizing I was working on an essay and tiptoeing through my office.

My parents, Clifton Fadiman and Annalee Whitmore Jacoby Fadiman, were both alive when I started this book but died before I finished. Their influence is as strong as ever.

My husband, George Howe Colt, and I spent hundreds of hours in bed, under the watchful gaze of the wooden birds I wrote about in "Night Owl," debating the relative merits of various word choices. "Summary" or "essence"? "Inspect" or "keep tabs"? "Exceptional" or "superlative"? "Imperishable" or "inextinguishable"? The essence of our relationship is the way he keeps tabs on my words and my life, both superlatively, as a result of which my love and gratitude are inextinguishable.

Kim Fadiman, to whom *At Large and At Small* is dedicated, has been the co-curator of the Serendipity Museum of Nature, my companion on many memorable wilderness trips, and, for fifty-three years, an incomparable brother. We talked endlessly about each of these essays, just as we had talked endlessly about luna moths and pickled tapeworms when we were children. We no longer collect nature, but Kim is still my favorite person with whom to watch it, preferably before making, and then eating, a batch of liquid nitrogen ice cream.